A Millennial's Topsy-Turvy Chase for Gainful Employment; or,
A Generation's Catalog of Conundrums

Kristin D. Butler

The Cats Be Unemployed

Copyright © 2018 by Kristin D. Butler.

Library of Congress Control Number:		2017904994
ISBN:	Hardcover	978-1-5434-1263-5
	Softcover	978-1-5434-1261-1
	eBook	978-1-5434-1262-8

All rights reserved. No part of this book may be reproduced or transmitted in any form or by any means, electronic or mechanical, including photocopying, recording, or by any information storage and retrieval system, without permission in writing from the copyright owner.

This book is part memoir. It reflects the author's present recollections of experiences over time. Some names and characteristics have been changed, some events have been compressed, and some dialogue has been recreated.

Although the author has made every effort to ensure that the information in this book was correct at press time, the author and publisher do not assume and hereby disclaim any liability to any party for any loss, damage, or disruption caused by errors or omissions, whether such errors or omissions result from negligence, accident, or any other cause.

The author has made every effort to cite sources in this work. If, for any reason, a source is not cited or is attributed incorrectly, please contact the author, so that updates can be made accordingly.

Contact: thecatsbeunemployed@gmail.com

Print information available on the last page.

Rev. date: 03/01/2018

To order additional copies of this book, contact:
Xlibris
1-888-795-4274
www.Xlibris.com
Orders@Xlibris.com
759930

Contents

Chapter 1: The Cats Be Unemployed 1

Young, educated, and un(der)employed after the Great Recession.

Chapter 2: Finding A Job… Any Job! 13

Job application grievances for college grads.

Chapter 3: You Might Be Unemployed If… 27

Humorous musings on unemployed life.

Chapter 4: Precarious Positions 35

Working in jobs run by questionable people and policies, and the precarious positions I found myself in.

Chapter 5: Fast Cash 49

Viable and not-so-viable gig work; my weird experiences from Craigslist.

Chapter 6: Is This A Scam? 64

Working for a company that may have been a scam.

Chapter 7: The Disconnects 84

A look at how education and real world application are not fully aligned.

Chapter 8: College Issues (Cost and Value) 99

> *The deep issues and questions surrounding higher education's cost and value.*

Chapter 9: Family Roomies 129

> *Recollections of living at home as a twentysomething.*

Chapter 10: 94 To 100 Degrees Or Bust! 143

> *A desperate attempt to pass a pre-screening drug test.*

Chapter 11: The Daily Deal Downfall 151

> *Working for a start-up "copycat" company and witnessing its downfall.*

Chapter 12: Baiting The Unemployed 162

> *Living on unemployment benefits; discovering how job seekers can be deceived.*

Chapter 13: Wage Rage! 172

> *A look at the minimum wage and job creation in our society.*

Chapter 14: Broke And Broken 183

> *The effects that unemployment, dead end jobs, and being broke had on my relationships.*

Chapter 15: Get This Headset Off Of Me! 193

> *A media sales call center fiasco.*

Chapter 16: Currently Seeking: Perfection 205

> *The truth behind working with recruiters; the hidden meaning behind job board posts.*

Chapter 17: Health Care Conditions 215

> *The state of health care in America and how the Affordable Care Act impacted women and young adults.*

Chapter 18: Shafū 241

> *Working for a foreign company with a strange dynamic; discussions on company culture (shafū).*

Chapter 19: Coming Of Age With Social Media And Rapid Technology 254

> *A look into the social and technological forces that shaped the Millennial generation and redefined what it means to be "grown up."*

Chapter 20: Quarter Life Crisis 262

> *Lost and confused as an aspiring adult, but learning to grow.*

About The Author 273

Acknowledgements 275

Bibliography 277

To all the lost cats out there trying to find their way in this crazy, mixed-up world!

All artwork by Noh A.

behance.net/Noh-a

Chapter 1

The Cats Be Unemployed

"Cats possess so many of the same qualities as some people that it is often hard to tell the people and the cats apart."

P.J. O'Rourke

A few years into my post-college life I found myself at a hip-hop concert for an underground artist, even though I usually listened to alternative and indie rock. I was open to new experiences, and the tickets were cheap. It was the summer of 2012 and my then-boyfriend and I were both 25, and recently laid off, unemployed college graduates. We were doing what we could to pass the time until our next job opportunity.

As the beats pumped throughout the outdoor venue, I wandered aimlessly through the rowdy crowd, sticky from the summer heat, trying to find a place to cool down. On my way to grab a drink, I stumbled across a table with T-shirts and other band paraphernalia. A bright yellow shirt with a cartoon cat lying atop some Chinese characters caught my eye. Above the Chinese letters were the English words: "The Cat Be Unemployed."

I smirked, and suddenly I felt simpatico with the cat.

Cats are similar to the unemployed young adults of today. Cats are called self-centered, aloof and lazy. Cats are accused of ignoring others. Cats sleep the days away. Cats don't have to put on pants or take showers. Cats mooch for free rent or food. Cats are curious of their surroundings. Cats are cautious of their next steps. Cats are constantly put in boxes. Cats hate closed doors.

We bought the shirt. I was curious, though: where did this quirky T-shirt idea come from? I did what any inquisitive, technically savvy person would do: I Googled it.

Shirt by designer Klughaus for Despot the hip hop artist

I learned that in 2011, 12 people were arrested in New York for smuggling and selling illegal pesticides—illegal because this rat poison was 61 times more potent than the government allows. Why? To put a monopoly on the business? To get rid of colonies of abnormally gigantic mice? To make extra cash in troubling times? Who knows! The rat poison came in a yellow and blue box with the same drawing and words on it as the tee shirt.[1]

The cat image suddenly made sense to me. I thought, so the rats be dead because of innovations in poison, and the cats are left without a job to do? *The cat unemployment rate must be absurd!*

But hey, it turns out there is hope for the cats! One of the first stories I found in the course of my search was about the San Antonio Country Club, who in 2012 hired a team of previously unemployed felines to rid the property of mice, giving the feral cats the rare opportunity to become productive members of society. I found similar stories of cats working in bookstores, breweries, coffee shops, vet offices, train stations, hospitals, and some were even promoted to "mayors" of towns. Some kitties have taken the Internet and social media by storm and are earning money. Poison replaced most of the cats' more traditional jobs, but these felines still found a way.

Are young adults similar to the cats, just looking for an opportunity to do what we do best in a world of ever-changing options? Does that mean we Millennial "cats" can find a way, too? We are persistent, persuasive and peculiar. In many ways, the members of this generation are like adult cats in that we can probably make it on our own, but we need someone (friends, family, mentors and leaders) to look out for us now and again.

You're born, you grow up, and then you have to find a way to earn money or be a productive part of society; it's an unavoidable clause in the contract of life. Generation Y, also known as the Millennial Generation, has grown up in an era where finding a decent job has been challenging due to a recession that largely hit in 2008.

I started out at community college and then excitedly moved up to a Texas private university. I graduated in 2009 after studying and practicing journalism and sociology. I was so pumped by the fact that I had earned a degree, I proudly walked across that stage and clung to my expensive piece of paper. I am grateful for my college experience and that my supportive family and friends helped me get through college, and also came to see me dressed in my purple cap and gown on graduation day. But I entered a world in a weak economy, where finding a decent job would be as difficult as herding cats, and suddenly I became a poignant example of youth un(der)employment. Instead of gaining a decent job out of college as one would hope, I built up experience being "professionally unemployed." I found myself without a job six times within a five year span. When I actually was working, it was in jobs that did not require a degree, or in no way related to my studies in college, or did not pan out to be the stepping stone I yearned for.

Many of us did everything we were supposed to do on the checklist for success we were given: Graduate from high school. Figure out what we want to be when we grow up. Go to college. Work internships. Volunteer. Gain knowledge and experience. Graduate college. But then what happens? We have a piece of paper that many can argue makes us... average? We struggle financially, physically and mentally. We struggle to find a job worth doing... or any job, for that matter. We start out working for around minimum wage, which is nearly nothing... learning that, indeed, nothing is guaranteed.

Many young people today know how difficult it is to find a good job. We also know the playing field has changed, but many still ponder why. We do not have any personal experience from past job markets to compare it to. It's like, okay, we know this isn't how it's always been, so how did the tables turn on America's young adults? Where did all the jobs go? What happened to the economy?

There are many reasons for the tank of the economy. One of the most talked about reasons for the recession was due to a combination of Wall Street behavior, low interest rates, and safe-harbor rules for investing in high-risk debt. It all sent investments pouring into real estate in the early 2000's. Criteria were loosened for mortgage loans, and as a result many non-fixed rate, sub-prime loans were written to people with low income and bad credit. Then, a bunch of questionable and risky behavior went down in the bundling and selling of mortgages in consolidation packages to other finance companies, without properly rating the riskiness of the loans in the packages. When interest rates eventually went up on those loans, the banks and financial firms became aware that the loan packages they bought contained bad apples. They found themselves in danger of going bankrupt once they realized most of the sub-prime loans were at risk of defaulting.[i] There was too much debt that was not able to be paid back on those sub-prime loans. The Federal government had to bail the banks out of trouble, with taxpayer money. The loss of wealth led to sharp cutbacks in bank lending, business investing, and consumer spending. U.S. housing prices fell and the stock market took a nose dive. International trade dropped, credit card debt soared, unemployment rose, and hiring froze. From late 2007 to mid- 2009, the U.S. labor market lost approximately 8.7 million jobs.[2] The era of the "Great Recession" began, which was named due to a sharp decline in economic activity around the world. It is loosely compared by many economists to the "Great Depression" of the 1930's.

The aftermath and effects of the Great Recession are still felt by many, even a decade later. While we have seen recovery, it has been slow. The economy's gross domestic product (GDP: total dollar value of all goods and services produced over a specific time period) has only averaged 2.1 percent annual growth over the years after the recession.[3]

---

[i] I recommend the movies *Inside Job* (2010) and *The Big Short* (2015) for an informative and entertaining understanding of the lead up to the Great Recession.

In addition to companies and the government having to cut jobs due to budget crunches in the face of economic predicaments, there are a multitude of other reasons why the workforce landscape has changed. U.S. businesses are bombarded with regulations and taxes, making it hard for many businesses to stay afloat. In 1936, the number of pages in the *Federal Register* was about 2,600. Today, it's over 80,000 pages long. The *Federal Register* is a way for the government to announce changes to government requirements, policies and guidance to the public. More and more rules and regulations are added or revised all the time, and many of those rules—taxes, registrations, permits and compliance issues—affect businesses.

Gen Y has seen companies that we grew up with file for bankruptcy, close down locations, or both. We have seen magazines fold, airlines shut down, and outdated tech companies lose their edge. Some of the more popular companies remembered by Millennials to undergo these tribulations include Blockbuster, Virgin Megastore, Circuit City, RadioShack, Napster, Sears, K-Mart, Borders, Delia's, KB Toys, Linens 'n Things, American Apparel, Payless and SkyMall.

Competition for the desirable job openings that are actually available is fierce. Businesses have struggled to afford to keep their current employees, and young people (with and without college degrees) have been forced to compete for career openings with more experienced candidates who have, themselves, been suddenly put out of a job. And since the domestic demand for jobs has gone up, starting pay has gone down, as companies know they can find someone willing to work for lower pay.

Older workers are also prolonging retirement for personal or financial reasons, creating stagnancy in the workplace. As a result, nearly half of the nation's unemployed are under the age of 34.[4] According to Gallup, an American research-based consulting company, for the entire 18 to 29-year-old age bracket, the full-time employment rate is on the decline. In June, 2012, 47 percent of that entire age group had a full-time job. One year later, in June, 2013, only 43.6 percent of that entire age group had a full-time job.[5] That's a lot of us either working part time, not working at all, and not living up to our potential. The economic consequences of high unemployment in the young adult age range are enduring; failing to employ young people today will likely result in lost earnings, greater social costs, and slower economic growth tomorrow.

Rapid advances in technology result in innovations like Artificial Intelligence (robots and computers) taking over jobs that people used to perform. Cashiers, librarians, freight stockers, travel agents and phone operators are examples. Technology not only kills jobs, but it creates them too. New types of companies and jobs are being created all the time, but educators and people struggle to keep up with advancements in technology to fill new roles in industries such as electronics, the automotive sector, renewable energy, skilled systems, and robotics.

Throughout history, the transition into the labor market after college graduation has been difficult. High unemployment amongst new graduates is not a new phenomenon. Finding a good job has always been a grueling process. What is new is that the recession made it more difficult, and many college graduates are spending months to years unemployed, or holding part-time jobs, or even performing jobs that do not require a degree, and are therefore finding it difficult to pay back school loans. College graduates nowadays are taking longer to find financial freedom than previous generations. The cost of college continues to rise, yet it is questionable whether the value of a higher degree is equal to the money and time spent earning it. It's also seemingly more difficult for those *without* college degrees to find secure careers and become gainfully employed.

Of those young grads that are employed, many are working in roles for which they're "overqualified." It's reported by the Census Bureau that more people are going to college than ever before. But the job market is so cat eat cat because more of us have degrees and more of us need to compete!

A 2014 study done by the Department of Education on the lives of 13,133 27-year-olds intrigued me.[6] This was the exact same age I was ten years out of high school. It turns out, *only* 20 percent of us made more than $40,000 a year! On less than $40,000 a year, with expenses that could include rent, utilities, a cell phone, student loans, a car payment, car insurance, health insurance, and food, you pretty much need every penny. It leaves very little, if any, left over to put into a savings account. More than 84 percent of those 27-year-olds have some college education. A third of us have a bachelor's degree. But yet, 40 percent of the age group spent some time unemployed.

People say the Millennial generation is lazy and entitled, that we lack motivation, or that we expect everything to be handed to us. They say the reasons for our problems are that we majored in the "wrong" subject, or we were praised and instilled with a false sense of entitlement, or that we are not willing to work hard enough. But these reasons do not apply to every single person in my generation, and believing these statements is ignorant. Millennials do want a chance to succeed and work hard. People say, "Pull yourself up by the bootstraps!" or, "Stop complaining and go make a living!" But many Millennials don't want to whine about the socioeconomic landscape that is in front of us. We want to change it. We want to make a difference. It's definitely hard to focus on making a difference when we are responsible for paying off major debt caused by inflating college costs, while simultaneously battling an upside-down job market and ever increasing housing prices.

I experienced firsthand a number of aspects of being young, college-educated, and hopelessly un(der)employed. I lived at home with my parents into my late twenties, received unemployment paychecks, and blindly applied to hundreds of jobs. I also got myself into some precarious situations on my path to find financial freedom. I worked odd jobs to pay my student loans, got laid off multiple times, found myself without health insurance, witnessed scams and questionable company cultures, and pulled myself out from the rubble after the downfall of a start-up company. My efforts to find gainful employment came with other life challenges, too, including family health struggles, rocky relationships affected by the stress of jobs and growing pains, and my own "quarter life crisis." As hard as I aimed for financial independence, I couldn't seem to catch that juicy fish.

How has our socioeconomic landscape changed for young people since the recession? What are young people going through to find jobs? What is the workplace like now for young adults? Are students being adequately prepared for the real world? Is college worth it? Does it take some of us longer to grow up and find where we belong? Are we disillusioned with society? Can changes be made to help current and future generations? Are we holding ourselves accountable? Some of these questions have answers. Others just generate more questions.

This book, a hybrid of sorts, blends research, personal reflection, and humor to examine the challenges young adults encounter constantly.[ii] I have experienced, discussed with peers, and done an extensive amount of fact-finding to examine what is happening with my generation. As a result, I question many aspects of society, the working world, and education. I aim to relate my stories (and those close to me with some names changed) to the bigger picture. These are the hard truths I discovered and the lessons I learned during the topsy-turvy chase to find gainful employment.

After everything I've been through, I realize that some parts of society have the potential to be different. It's not all doom and gloom. With enough patience and effort, we can persevere, individually and collectively. I know that my opinions and ideas are not going to be accepted by everyone.

[ii] As Princess Unikitty from *The Lego Movie* would say, we are going to talk some "business, business, business, numbers!"

Unlike actual cats, people don't like to be placed in boxes. I don't have all the answers, nor do I claim to. I aim to entertain, inform, and perhaps sometimes have something wise to say! But by all means, I encourage everyone to think of innovative ideas and solutions to the conundrums facing aspiring young adults today.

Of course, some of my mishaps were completely my fault, while others were outside my control. Many may not agree with the decisions I made when placed in desperate situations, but I take full responsibility for my actions and have learned from my mistakes. I am not here to blame anyone for my decisions or my life trajectory. Not all my misfortunes were solely catalyzed by larger economic forces, but these stories are representative of the kinds of setbacks that anyone could endure in the job market today, while on the quest for independence. I do hope you can relate to, or at least enjoy my candor about what it's like to be young, educated, and feeling like a lost, stray cat, wandering down the wrong alley.

Chapter 2

Finding A Job... Any Job!

On a break from the job search a couple of years out of college, I found myself hanging at a neighborhood pool with my friends, Alec and Peter, on a hot Texas summer day. As we kicked back and enjoyed the sunshine, we watched a bunch of kids in the water playing games and horsing around. One of the older kids shouted out to the younger kids, "Who wants to be young forever!?"

"Me! Me!! Me!!" they all responded.

My friend Peter, who was only 24 at the time, also responded with a big, hearty *"ME!!!"*

The kids just laughed and laughed, and the boy who'd asked the question in the first place proclaimed, "Good one, sir!"

Sir!? I couldn't help but look at my friend and feel boggled at the word "sir" being applied to him. As I laughed along with everyone else at the situation, I realized that even if we want to, it's impossible to stay young forever. At some point we must grow up, decide what we want to do with our lives, and figure out how to pay the bills. As much as we were still young at heart, entry into the "real world" was upon us.

Pew[iii] Research's "2012 Social & Demographic Trends Project," which surveyed 2,048 adults nationwide, outlined just how hard it has been for 18 to 34-year-olds to adjust to the real world. Almost half of us have taken a menial job just to pay the bills, almost a quarter have worked without pay to get experience, and more than a third have gone back to school because we can't find employment. But the job front is just the beginning. The survey also found that the weak economy is leaving a mark on young people's personal lives, changing our futures in big ways: almost one-third delayed marriage or having a baby, and almost a quarter moved back home with parents.[7] The report was all too real to me. I was experiencing and witnessing what was being reported all around me. The idea that having a college degree was the main requirement to find a good job was simply proving to be false.

As I applied for hundreds of jobs after college, I realized how difficult it was to find an entry-level position at a reputable company. Many jobs readily available are not the sort that a college graduate sees as a budding career. There are an abundance of employment opportunities working in sales or call centers, serving tables, driving trucks, doing gig work, or working an unpaid, part-time internship just to gain some experience and get a paw in the door. We are told that the best way to obtain a job is to establish connections, network with people you know, and have a focus — *what is it that we really want to do?* Yes, it's helpful to use who and what

---

[iii] There's going to be a lot of these. Pew pew... pew pew pew!!!

you know, but not everyone has connections. Many of us end up having to sort through a lot of kitty litter to get past all the crappy jobs out there. Even when I tried to connect with the people I knew in my field, they often did not have any work available, or the opportunity was not what I thought it would be, or, discouragingly, they would not even reply to my e-mails.

Gone are the days when a college education entitles a person to a certain salary. But so many people of all ages are still convinced that graduating from high school, going to college to get a bachelor's degree, or maybe even a master's, will guarantee a lifelong career with good pay. The third annual online "College Graduate Employment Survey," which was conducted by Accenture Strategy and included about 2,000 college graduates from 2013, 2014, and 2015, shows disparities between career expectations and the reality of entry-level jobs.[8] Perhaps the most striking result was that more than half of the soon-to-be graduates thought they wouldn't have trouble finding a job, even though only 12 percent had one lined up. *Boy, what a reality check they had coming.* Yes, having a degree can help graduates move ahead on a list of job applicants, but there are no guarantees. It's still hard work learning how to set oneself apart and hone specific skills.

We are now competing with more qualified candidates for the same entry-level jobs. I found that even when I followed the extensive job hunting advice I found online, there was no perfect formula for getting invited to an interview. Even when I made my best efforts to be personable and professional, I was left wondering why I didn't land the opportunity. *What could I have done better, or differently?* Besides the fact that it can take hours just to find *one* job that you are a) interested in, b) qualified for, c) in the right location for, and d) a good fit for, some employers still feel the need to make us jump through hoops just to get a resume on their computer screens. Even if you're lucky enough to have someone open and review your resume, there's no guarantee of an interview since it's difficult to convey who you are through your CV[iv] alone. Employers receive hundreds of resumes for the jobs they post, so they can be overwhelmed and easily overlook an application if they find even one thing they do not like. *Oops, copied and pasted a previously used cover letter, and sent it off without changing the company name—can forget about getting that job!*

You would think given the rise of the Internet and other advances in technology, and that we no longer need to scour newspaper ads, apply in person, or actually wait in line at the unemployment counter, it would actually be easier than ever to apply for a job. Studies have shown that, while the Internet reduces time spent looking for work by 25 percent, it does not make jobs easier to obtain.[9] Some employers make it difficult to even apply. While some employers still care about their potential employees and make submitting a resume straightforward, professional, and easy, some employers make applying to one single job time consuming. Many company websites made me a) sign up for an account with a username, b) ID number, c) strong password, d) secret questions in case I forgot my username or password, and e) take a personality questionnaire—all before I could even start the process of applying for open positions.

[iv] AKA Cat Vita!

As I have found myself on the job hunt multiple times, I will give you some examples of the hassles of applying to jobs through the Internet for a college grad in this competitive world. *(Warning: Waggish humor ahead.)*

How it feels to write a cover letter:

To whom it may concern,

> *(Jumping up and down with a flashing sign)*
> *Hello there!! Hi hi, hi hi hi!!!! Did I get your attention yet?*
> *Pick me! Pick me! Dammit! Pick me!*

Or...

> *Dear Hiring Manager,*
>
> *I swear this is original, and not a copy and paste, of say, all the other cover letters I have been slinging around the black hole of the Internet...*
> *Here I am, trying to make a mark by showing you on a boring piece of paper everything I learned by earning my fancy piece of paper. But I am not just a piece of paper! I'm real. Check it out, we are only three connections away on LinkedIn. Can we just count that as a reference?*

I would like to work for your company because, well, you are hiring! Hooray! Your company needs a new employee... I can be that new employee, whatever that entails! What are you looking for? Someone creative? Techy? Spunky? A Ninja? I do have cat like reflexes... I am actually good at a multitude of things, like putting up with a ton of crap! Plus I have a charming personality. Hire me! ☺

I have feelings, hopes and aspirations. I want to put in hard work. I want to make a difference. I want people to see me for what I have to offer. I feel I am turning grey and worn as each day passes, as I wait for someone to give me a chance.

Hmm... I know! I am attaching a picture of myself. Do you see the wrinkles and salt and pepper hair I edited in? Does this make me seem more seasoned?

I only hope for a lick of your time to prove to you that I do have the mindset and willpower to be the go-getting tiger you are looking for. No, I didn't mean I would actually lick you. Unless... Never mind... Darn it, why am I so awkward? And now I am so tired from racking my brain to try to be original, I am going to pass out on this keyboard. Here's hoping I don't get lost in oblivion. Call me, maybe!?

Hopeful college graduate

Drooling ensues

How it feels to get a letter back after submitting a resume:

Dear Candidate,

We will now begin your application process for the entry-level job that requires three to five years of experience, a phenomenon that will never make sense. Please complete this five-page job application. Upload your resume, original cover letter, and five professional references, AND fill out this custom form that includes everything you already have on your resume. We just want you to re-supply all the information you've already filled out elsewhere in the application process so we know how serious and excited you really are about applying for a job that offers less money than your student loans cost to pay back. After all, hundreds of other candidates will be applying for this position, and we want to ensure you have what it takes to be bossed around. Please provide your salary requirements, even though you have no idea how much you're worth, and we will automatically delete your application if you state something that is too high or not at all relevant. We only want to pay you as little as possible. In fact, this job may be commission only. We haven't decided yet. We might decide that we don't need to fill this position at all, or that the job description is completely different from the one you applied for.

Next, you must take this personality aptitude test that in no way reflects who you really are. On a scale of 1 to 5, how desperate are you? Next, you must take this intelligence test that will include questions that no one knows the answers to and that are not relevant to this job at all. "Ship: Harbor :: Our Application: Your Ass!" If you get through these rounds you will then submit to a background check... and, of course, you will only hear back from us in the unlikely event that we are interested in interviewing you.

Thank you for your time. We know you have a lot of it.

Sincerely,
Crapola Company

How it feels to get a rejection letter:

Dated 6 months after applying:

Dear Candidate,

Thank you for your application to Crapola Company. You may have already forgotten you applied here given how much time has passed. We appreciate your experience and interest in working for us. Unfortunately, we have decided to move forward with another candidate. We are, in fact, so ridiculous in our hiring practices that we use software and third party job application websites, which pretty much guarantees you will be rejected. No humans are involved on our end, just robots. Boop bop beep bop! These websites and software are like virtual wastebaskets for your resume. Please do not respond to this e-mail, as this account is not monitored.

Best of luck in your future endeavors,

Crapola Company

How it feels to get an interview invitation:

Dear Candidate,

Congratulations! You must be good at jumping through fire, because you made it to the interview! You are 50 percent of the way there! Now all you have to do is dress to impress, spend hours researching the company, and knock us dead with your outstanding personality. We may ask you questions like, "Tell me about yourself," or, "What is your biggest weakness?" But we may also ask you irrelevant questions like, "What kitchen utensil would you be?" or, "How many cows could fit in this room?" We may say that you will be required to work and constantly be on the phone from 7:30 am to 7:30 pm every day. Then we may ask you, with a straight face, if you could see yourself being excited about this opportunity. You will be required to lie through your smiling teeth, because of course you can't tell the truth. We might brag about how awesome it is to work for Crapola Company. The cat's pajamas! We may list how many awards we have achieved, and how happy our employees are, but in actuality we are an under-paying company that is only interested in a workhorse. We may tell you that you would also need to provide your own laptop and cell phone in the unlikely event that we actually hire you. We might even have three interviews with you, and still not offer you a job. Sorry about that.

Best,

Crapola Company

Sometimes a person on a job hunt can feel about as productive as a cat chasing after a laser pointer. While on my job hunts, I kept an Excel file of every single job I applied for, and the results of each application. I found that out of every 25 jobs I applied for, approximately one to two would reply back, if I was lucky.

Getting an automated message back may seem like an annoyance or a let-down, but the most disgruntling aspect of the whole experience is that the majority of employers don't even reply back. We never hear a word from them. During and after the Great Recession, the news reported that employers often cut down their administrative and HR teams to save money. This means that instead of being screened by live people, many candidates are screened by automated bots, and are rejected from potential jobs just because resumes are not written in a way that the computer recognizes as fit. If a hiring manager actually talked to the person, the company would more easily identify who might be a fit, but to get past the automated system is a job in itself! If hiring managers want the person interviewing to take the job seriously, then why do some make applying such a joke?

I found, in my searches, that good jobs are out there, but most require beating out stiff competition and possibly accepting pay lower than anticipated. According to *The New York Times*, and research based on past large recessions, college grads who graduated and kicked off the job search in 2009[v], or shortly after, are likely to experience pay ten to 15 percent lower than slightly older peers, and for as long as a decade after leaving school.[10] Graduating in a tough economy may take a chunk from your paycheck for what seems like the short term, but it can take years to recover the loss. Employers often look at past salaries when researching

---

[v] Coincidently, 2009 is the year I graduated from college. Drats!

candidates and a low starting pay may keep some candidates underpaid well into our careers, an unfair process that many say should be an illegal practice. Many of my peers and I learned that no one is going to pay a $50,000 starting salary to someone with minimum skills or experience. Sometimes you do have to find a job... *any job*... just to get the ball rolling.

Many employers want people they can hire right away, who can do the job without any sort of job-specific training or education. The Association of American Colleges and Universities found that employers feel college graduates are not prepared for jobs.[11] Employers struggle to find the right type of qualified candidates, even though hundreds of people compete for the same position. *There must be a few of us who have the skills, or at least the capability to learn to do the job, right?*

Application requirements can include a laundry list of prerequisites, to the point where employers are unlikely to find any individual who fits *every single* skill they want. Employers are looking for candidates who are already in similar positions to the job they're applying for, or already working for a similar company. I sometimes felt like not only did they want me to be the chef, they also wanted me to be the farmer! This often scares off good, qualified people who think that since they are missing a few skills from the employer's list that they simply are not qualified and must, therefore, apply for jobs that are beneath their skill level. On the other hand, those people who apply to jobs way beyond their qualifications adds to the disarray of the system.

Many of us are self-taught. Technology has made people more competent, or at least has made it easier to access information right away. Meanwhile, schools are not necessarily teaching all of the skills employers are looking for. Going to college costs a lot of money, and much of the information we may use for our jobs is available for free. Many of us can slyly admit to Googling "how to_____" during the first few months on the job.

Employers may also feel that young adults do not have the right presence in interviews; that we seem to not take the process seriously. If we take getting a job seriously, then we must do our best to prepare interview questions and responses, research the company history and culture, and prepare a professional outfit to wear. Okay, so we know not to show up empty-brained, in a Grateful Dead tee, reeking of smoke, smacking bubble gum, with our mom tagging along for moral support. But shouldn't the same be said for the interviewer? I once showed up to an interview dressed in a brand new outfit, and had even practiced interview questions in front of the mirror, only to find that my interviewer had not even reviewed my resume and was wearing distressed jeans and flip-flops. *Cowabunga dude!* No, I wasn't applying to work in a surf shop.

What I have learned from the tedious job application process is that you need to have some sort of vision. Walking blindly though the application phase will only get you lost along the way. It's important to have some goals in mind for the industry you want to work in, type of job you want to acquire, and to use the keywords hiring managers (and bots) are looking for on your resume. And even though it can be quite difficult, writing a personal, well thought out cover letter can be worth the time to help you stand out. Just flinging resumes everywhere isn't effective.

The job application process is rough, and the interview process can be both mind-numbing and scary. I learned that I had to fall on my butt a lot, but eventually, with the right efforts, I learned to land on my feet, *just like a cat always does*. I learned that the job application process is about focusing on growth and opportunity, even if it doesn't always result in the "perfect job." We can't let the ridiculous system defeat us!

Chapter 3

You Might Be Unemployed If...

Unemployed? You're not alone . . .

Statistics understate the real percentage of unemployment. Generation Opportunity, a national, non-partisan youth advocacy organization, announced that in May 2014, about six years after the recession hit, the unemployment rate was 9.1 percent for those 18 to 29-years-old.[12] The numbers we see in the news reflect those who are actually looking for full-time work, not those who have given up or need to take a short break from the work force. If you are no longer eligible for unemployment benefits because your allocated time ran out, you no longer count in the statistics. If you have been without work and only sporadically searching for a job, not actively looking, then you are not considered unemployed nor employed. If you found a part time job, but didn't take it because you actually needed full-time employment... you don't count either. It does not count those who are working part-time while still looking for a "real job." With more people retiring, going back to school, or simply giving up on the job hunt, millions and millions of Americans are not counted in the unemployment rate.

What should we consider ourselves if we are neither employed or unemployed? *Le sigh…* Are we just damn cats that sit around licking our toes??

Generation Opportunity estimates that the real percentage of young adults within ages 18 to 29 who are without a job is 15.5 percent. To put this in perspective, there are an estimated 53.7 million people between 18 to 29-years-old.[13] That would mean there are about 8.3 million budding minds without full-time work! On top of that, the Federal Reserve estimates that 44 percent of college grads in their twenties are stuck in low-wage, dead-end jobs, which is the highest rate in decades.[14]

As you take time to realize exactly what it is you want and need out of a job, it usually means spending a lot of time on job boards, networking, perfecting your resume or LinkedIn profile, or, more likely, trying to find ways to escape reality. When you are young and un(der)employed, it's easy to find yourself doing peculiar things that older people, or people with established careers, or even you yourself, find weird. You may end up in humorous or desperate situations. You might even go through a variety of strange emotions.

You might be unemployed if . . .

- You used to get jealous of your cat or dog every time you left for work. Now the two of you stare at each other all day while sitting in awkward positions on the couch.

- You watched all seven seasons of *Weeds* on Netflix in two and a half weeks. You start taking notes on Nancy's networking skills.
- You go to the grocery store or Target in the middle of the day and wonder what the hell everyone else there does for a living.
- You finally have time to go to doctors' appointments… but oops… no insurance! You consider doing a dine-and-dash at Care Now when you get the flu.
- You decide you will read more, with all your free time, so you browse online for books. You end up with a cart full of shoes you can't afford, instead.
- Now that you don't have to worry about getting to work on time, you vow to finally start exercising in the mornings. Instead, you spend more time reading fitness magazines in bed… because staying in bed seems safer. At least you're reading now!
- You actually do some of the projects you spend all your time pinning on Pinterest. Turns out, those mop shoes you made work great! Plus, you now know how to cook chicken 147 ways!
- You start couponing to keep a better budget. You finally understand those crazy coupon ladies when you see the great deals you're getting. Then you realize you have to buy 20 barbecue sauces to get them all for a penny each. It doesn't even matter that you know 147 ways to cook chicken, because all you will be eating is the barbecue variety.
- You endorse people for skills on LinkedIn, even though you have never met in real life, in hopes they will endorse you too.

- You sleep all the time, often at odd hours. You constantly feel tired and take cat naps, only to wake up just in time for that pre-screening interview.
- You cross your fingers every time you swipe your credit card, hoping it's not going to be rejected. Just like your resume has been for months.
- When people ask how your job search is going, all you want to do is give them the death stare of Grumpy Cat, then nonchalantly knock a random object off the table and slowly walk away.
- You frequent coffee shops in hopes of being more productive in your job search, but end up dreaming of becoming part of a romantic comedy where your future lover accidently grabs for your coffee at the same time you do. You brush hands, eyes meet, and BOOM! It's love at first sight! The two of you can share a muffin and recommend self-improvement books to each other!
- You try to become more cultured by seeing local plays and music performances, but all it does is cause you to feel like you should spend more time being artistic instead of sleeping all the time.
- You find yourself baking excessively. Who cares if you put on a few extra pounds? It's not like you leave the house that often anyways. That would require putting on pants. Or a bra!
- You break open your piggy bank and begin verbally harassing everyone who ever gave you an IOU... that kid from middle school who "borrowed" some quarters for the soda machine? Time to pay up, Kevin!!

- You become envious of others on Facebook and wish you were just as happy in your work and personal life as they are. You angrily delete your Facebook profile, only to reactivate it hours later because you've run out of online personality quizzes to take.
- Your $80,000 diploma is collecting dust. You're too bitter to clean it.
- You Google "quarter life crisis" and question your whole life trajectory. Wait, you're already more than a quarter of the way through life and you haven't even thought about a 401K yet!?
- You go days without showering. It's good for your hair, right?
- You drank too much with your service industry friends and are throwing up... on a Tuesday!
- You wear a sarcastic "Sorry For Partying" shirt... on a Wednesday!
- You actually are not sure what day of the week it is. Is it Caturday?
- You get so stressed you find yourself pooping, a lot. Or maybe it's all the cheap ramen you have been eating...
- You feel depressed so to cheer yourself up you put on a fox tail and prance around doing a little dance that involves a lot of butt shaking. You name it the "Foxy Dance." [vi]
- You update your voicemail to inform recruiters you are no longer accepting new opportunities because they won't stop calling you for commission based sales jobs no one wants. Your friends leave you messages pretending to offer you the role of a lifetime.

[vi] Maybe that's just me...

- You haven't filled up your gas tank in a month. It's not like you're driving to work every day. Hooray for saving money... and the environment!?

- You finally have time to attempt to break a Guinness World Record. I mean... when else are you going to be able to practice balancing pennies on your face? Or practice your loudest purr?

- Your favorite time of the day is when Ellen is on TV. You wish she would invite you onto her show and present you with a suitcase full of money to pay off all your student loans.

- You don't have money to buy drinks at the bar, so you master tricks and bet your friends to buy you a beer. Example: Bet that you can talk for a minute straight without using a word with the letter A in it. Solution: Count from 1-100, which takes about a minute. There are no A's in any of the numbers! (Okay, so you might get a slug to the shoulder and not a drink, but it's still fun!)

- You actually consider drinking someone's left behind, half-full, back-washed drink at the bar. Maybe you actually do it...

- You are too scared to check your bank account because you fear the wrath of the overdraft monster.

- You constantly create new e-mail accounts just to get the free month of Netflix or Amazon Prime. You be so sneaky...

- You scour your parent's house for loose change and random objects to sell for pennies, just so you have money for a bottle of $5 Andre to celebrate getting through another day. Plus you need extra pennies to keep practicing your balancing act.
- You spend way too much time creating memes and watching hilarious cat videos on YouTube. At least it keeps you from feeling depressed.
- Miss Kimberly "Sweet Brown" Wilkins proudly proclaims in her infamous YouTube video, "Ain't nobody got time for that!" You have watched it, laughing hysterically, about a hundred times because, well, you got a little time. And you're a little drunk from that Andre bottle.
- You start the project of researching your family history. You find out your great, great, great, grandfather made $8,000 a year! You are shocked at how little that is… and then you remember… it's more than you are making now!
- You volunteer at the local soup kitchen and stuff some bread in your pants for yourself because, hey, you're poor too.
- You are constantly on Craigslist trying to find non-degrading ways to make extra cash. This ad says he only wants to take pictures of belly buttons. That's not creepy, right?
- You start going dumpster diving in nice neighborhoods. This ally cat be finding deodorant, phone chargers, bagels and shirts for days!
- You used to think it could be "funemployment", but really, it has turned into the feeling of "bumemployment."

- You compare yourself to a cat. Living at home rent-free, not wearing pants, sleeping all day, going crazy, ignoring your parents, and only grooming yourself when you feel like it. You haven't shaved in weeks and you're beginning to wonder if you are actually turning into a fluffy cat. You sit around pawing at that mouse, always on the hunt. You find yourself endlessly bouncing around or running into walls. You bite your nails, while lying around waiting for something interesting to happen, often feeling like you want to go out, but you also just want to stay in...

Chapter 4

Precarious Positions

I didn't have a job lined up after college graduation in 2009. Most people I knew didn't. So I decided to take some time off. It was summer, after all, and I wanted to enjoy my last few months of real freedom. In retrospect, maybe it wasn't the greatest idea to put off finding a job. The recession at its peak combined with my little experience, made job hunting a wearisome experience. My first jobs ended up being either part-time or paying just above minimum wage. They also got me into some altercations with unprofessional people. Sure, finding a job is hard, but keeping it can be just as big of a struggle. Navigating problems in the workplace, it turns out, can be as tricky as a long-tailed kitty making its way through a room full of rocking chairs.

Part One: Distracted and Deceived

After month upon tedious month of sending out my resumes and cover letters, I started to feel nervous and discouraged, plucking at my eyebrows, watching the list of my applications grow and grow. I had applied to hundreds of positions, from entry-level marketing jobs to receptionist jobs, and sales jobs, to pretty much anything I thought I was remotely qualified for. I didn't hear back from most of them. I went on some interviews here and there, but nothing panned out. There were a few times when a job seemed promising, but then I would walk into the office building and be alarmed by the lack of furniture and people, not to mention the tiny size of the office space. *Do people actually work here? Would I actually want to work here?*

I finally got an interview for a part-time writer position at a small, local oil and gas company. I was desperate for anything at this point, since my bank account was dwindling. I met with the president (let's call him Mr. Slick) and his executive assistant at a restaurant near my house. It was the only interview in my life in which the employer fed me delicious food while asking about my background and skills. I thought, is this what grown up interviewing is like? *Pass the lettuce wraps, please!*

I determined the interview went well, and I was confident they were going to hire me. When I didn't hear back from them for a few weeks, I started to lose hope. I thought about working as a waitress for the time being, but it was hard to imagine clumsy me balancing trays of hot sticky food. Finally, a month after the interview, Mr. Slick got back to me and hired me part-time to run the company website and write their newsletter for investors. Feeling ecstatic, I jumped around and celebrated that I had finally found something—something that involved writing, no less! It was only part-time, but it was the highest paying job I had ever had up until that point. Since the job was only about 25 hours per week, I knew I would have to continue looking for a full-time job.

Unfortunately, other strife consumed my time and energy. During my senior year of college my mom developed melanoma, the deadliest form of skin cancer. She had never even used a tanning bed, so it came as a complete shock. But my whole family is fair-skinned, with freckles and moles, so our risk is higher than average. I remember the day she had me look at a discolored mole on her back. I took one look at the monster, and deep down, I knew it was cancer. I simply told her she needed to go get it removed and tested right away.

After I graduated college and moved back home, the cancer spread too close to her heart, so she underwent surgery to remove the mutated cells and have a port inserted for chemotherapy. In my family's experience, the chemotherapy treatment was worse than the cancer itself. I took my mother to chemo appointments a few times a week, where she would stay sitting in a chair for three hours at a time, in a room scattered with others going through similar treatments. Sometimes I would stay and keep her company, eating the provided cheese crackers and drinking Cola. Sometimes I had work to do, like driving my boss out to the oil field in his massive F-350 truck while hearing all about his suite at the Cowboys' stadium, or how he would take off in his private plane on weekends to explore oil ventures in other states.

As the months wore on, my mom aged what seemed like ten years. Her hair became extremely gray, thin and brittle. An old cane my sister and I had once used for playing dress-up now helped my mother get around. One day she became so faint, I could tell we needed to get her to the hospital so they could monitor her. The chemo treatment only gave her a 20 percent chance of never getting the cancer again, so after struggling through a few more months, the doctors gave her permission to quit treatment. It was only making her worse.

I was losing the fun woman I knew my mother as being. I wanted life to be normal again. I wanted my mother to be able and happy. I wanted my family to not have to worry so much about her. This consumed me and distracted me from trying to better my job situation.

Meanwhile, back at the office, whose staff consisted of only eight people, I found out truths about my boss through the whispering women around me. In the short few months I had been on board, I usually tried to mind my own business when I was actually in the office, but the rumors about Mr. Slick became hard to ignore. Questions about the legality of the oil and gas wells were thrown around. Status updates I was assigned to write for the investors didn't make sense to me based on what I actually saw in the field. The women in the office also said that Mr. Slick was cheating on his wife with his personal assistant. The two of them would often stay overnight in the towns where the oil and gas wells were located.

His personal assistant and I spent a lot of time together in the oil fields, sitting in the huge truck talking as we waited for the men to check the rate of gas or oil. We would work on our laptops or walk around in our rain boots checking out the sites, trying to ignore the catcalls from the oil drillers. She finally admitted to me that she had found this job in the "adult" section on Craigslist (which later was shut down). The ad (posted by Mr. Slick's executive assistant) guaranteed a job and a salary in return for services far beyond those of the average personal assistant. She told me she had taken the position because she was desperate for a job that could support her and her mentally disabled daughter. I wondered how long she went without decent pay before resorting to this last-ditch effort. How often did people have to succumb to any means possible just to pay the bills?

A few weeks later I needed to print a report on the front hall printer, and to do so, I needed to use the personal assistant's computer. She had not closed multiple tabs, and I could see that she was searching in the adult section, again, for other "opportunities." I couldn't believe how many men were looking for working sugar kittens. Of course, I kept my mouth shut since I was in serious need of a paycheck.

A few months down the road, Mr. Slick's wife decided she wanted to become more involved in her husband's business. Shortly after that, his pretty personal assistant was let go. The last I saw of her was making an angry exit out the back door, her bag flailing, dropping papers and an iPod behind her.

Mr. Slick's wife started asking me a lot of questions about my job. She said she wanted to start helping with the communications. She sent me e-mails asking for more information on what I actually did, and asked for samples of my work. Little by little, she started taking over my job, leaving me with little to nothing to do. I felt uneasy, and went home one day and cried, knowing the end of the job was coming soon. I cried not because I would miss the job, but because I was afraid of the unknown.

A few weeks later, Mr. Slick finally called me into the office and, as I had predicted, let me go. He simply told me it just "wasn't the right time" and compensated me with a "severance package." Unemployment was handed to me in the form of hush money.

That might have been the end of the precarious situations I had to experience there, but it was just the beginning of the demise of the company. A few months later, the Securities and Exchange Commission (SEC) filed suit in federal court alleging Mr. Slick and three other men whom I worked around had defrauded more than 300 investors out of millions of dollars in bogus oil and gas company promotion. Mr. Slick and his buddies had made cold calls, advertised on websites, and according to court records, told some prospective investors they could double or triple their initial investment. I had always wondered how they were able to keep collecting investors when the company's wells seemed to be more *miss* than *hit*. The wells, the SEC said, were extremely risky "wildcat" ventures with little proven potential.

The SEC said "sales" had told investors they would probably get their investment back within a couple of years. The SEC said that the projections were just speculative, and that the energy employee who formulated the payback had no oil and gas experience. Among those who lost their entire investment to the company was a fellow Millennial, a twentysomething blind man, who had handed over nearly $150,000 from his trust that was set up after the accident that blinded him.

It turns out the company had even more dirty secrets. The "sales" person I worked closely with had not only been lying to investors, he was a registered sex offender (and, incidentally, he had previously been the front man in an eighties rock band). My boss was a former used car salesman. *Talk about untrustworthy stereotypes.* Mr. Slick paid to cheat on his wife (the mother of his two children) and hid it on the company payroll, in addition to lying to people about the productivity of his company so he could cheat them out of their money. The thought of working at a company that had so many hidden secrets made me feel like I had been punched in the stomach over and over again.

Surprise, surprise, the company collapsed into bankruptcy in 2011. Mr. Slick and his wife also got divorced the same year. It turns out 2011 was a bad year for Mr. Slick. He had to return his company car, ended up crashing his company plane, and was sued by the Cowboys for unpaid balances on his suite.

Even after all of this, Mr. Slick moved up to a northern state and started a new oil drilling business. In the summer of 2012, newspapers reported that he and another conspirator illegally dumped hundreds of thousands of gallons (I'm talking close to a million) of toxic saltwater in an abandoned oil well, putting a cities' drinking water at risk and set a new record for the largest environmental violation fine ever in the state. After federal investigation, he was indicted in federal court with several felony charges including conspiracy to violate the Safe Drinking Water Act and defraud the United States. He was also charged with actually violating the Safe Drinking Water Act, making false statements, and obstructing grand jury proceedings. He will spend years in prison and owes more than fifteen million in fines.

It sickens me to have worked for a man that led a hoax on innocent people, and has no regard for people's safety or the environment. It's distressing to have been part of hiding lies from a broken family. My desperate need for a job and my own family issues kept me from seeing just how toxic the work environment was. It was after my employment that I became aware of all the schemes.

This beginning to my adulthood changed me. It woke me up quickly from the naive college student I had been and made me aware of the corruption that exists all around us. It made me realize just how immoral people and companies can be. It made me realize just how desperate people are to make a buck, especially in a bad economy. Choices led by anxiety due to financial situations can have a ripple effect in ways that are largely overlooked by society.

Part Two: The Power Of Words

My transfer from the oil fields to the unemployment field was quick, after only working for six months. My first job out of college had left a bad taste in my mouth, and I was unsure of my future. I didn't qualify for unemployment benefits because I had not been at my job long enough and it had only been part-time. At this point, I knew I needed work… and fast!

A month later, I began working for a popular department store, providing "customer service" at the registers. Some people also call this role "cashier." Sure, it wasn't a job that required a degree, but I tried to be optimistic. It was an established company, which counted for a lot after my first job experience out of college. The other employees were young and fun, and I got to be around fabulous clothes all day long. The employee discount didn't hurt either. I do take pride in finding good deals and making awesome outfits. I also got to be the voice of the store, with my message on the answering machine and my pipes echoing from the loudspeakers making store announcements in a smile through clenched teeth tone. *"Thank you for shopping with us today. It is our pleasure to serve you!"* I ranked as one of the top employees in opening new credit card accounts. On top of that, I had health insurance and my mother was finally declared cancer-free!

The problem with working at a popular retail store in your hometown is that eventually you have awkward encounters with people from your past. Old high school friends and frenemies, friends' cousins, moms of ex-boyfriends, neighbors and their little dogs, the person who sat behind you in College Lit, and the rich housewives from the gym flashing their gaudy diamond rings. EVERYONE! The world became smaller and smaller. I was 23, nearing 24, a college graduate, and embarrassed to be seen by people I knew, as I worked for slightly more than minimum wage.

Sometimes you could catch me ducking behind or into clothing racks, trying on sunglasses, or excusing myself to the bathroom to avoid running into people I knew. This was not what I went to school for, and this was not who I wanted to be. I didn't want people judging me for not living up to my potential. In retrospect, I should not have cared what others thought about me and my job. I knew it was temporary; I just wasn't sure what my next step was.

I learned I was not alone. A report called "The Idled Young Americans" found that the United States had gone from having the highest share of employed 25 to 34-year-olds among large, wealthy economies, to having among the lowest employed. The number of college grads working for minimum wage had doubled within a five-year period in the late 2000's. And since the minimum wage had not stayed up to date with inflation, many people make less than $20,000 a year, which makes it difficult to cover bills and loans.[15] I wondered how long it would take me to break away from the daily grind of living paycheck to paycheck.

Eight months into the retail job, I got dragged into a tricky situation. One of my best friends on the job, Senna, a quirky, quick-talking girl often made jokes that just fell off the tip of her tongue. One day she and I were in the break room and someone asked Senna to do her a favor, so she replied, *"Fo' shizzle, my nizzle!"* This is a term often used by Snoop Dogg and popularized in hip-hop culture. Three of the four people in the room didn't think anything of Senna's use of the silly phrase.

But one of our co-workers, a thirtysomething black woman who always seemed to want to pick arguments with people, blew up at Senna. She raged on about how Senna used inappropriate words and accused her of being malicious. She said something like, "Do you know what that word means!? That is the 'N' word! I will not stand for this!"

I proceeded to ask her to calm down; we didn't want a cat-fight. But she just hissed at me and huffed out of the room. We were all left standing there in a daze. We were shocked that something that seemed so minuscule could cause someone to feel so upset. Ignorantly, we did not correlate the word *nizzle* as slang for the 'N' word. If it were not for a quick search on Urban Dictionary, we might not have realized what the *fizzuck* she was talking about.

The next day I was called into the General Manager's office. I wasn't sure why I was summoned, but I had my suspicions. With my customer service manager in one chair and the GM in another, they asked me about the incident. I told the story exactly as it had happened, explaining that it was just a small faux pas, something Senna had said without realizing that it could offend someone. The two managers, both of whom were white, even admitted they had no idea what the word meant. But the GM accused me of lying about some details to cover for my friend. I was confused as to what I could have been lying about. I couldn't help but wonder what was different about my story versus the one told to the managers by the upset young woman. I felt like a silly cat that had gotten tangled in-between window blinds. I was in an uncomfortable precarious position. I still have no idea what the upset woman told the managers, but since the only other witness was out sick, they decided to take the upset woman's side.

The managers fired Senna to avoid the drama associated with a "racist incident." They didn't give my friend much of a chance. They also made me feel like a liar, even though I was completely honest about what had happened. Everything just blew out of proportion. Because most companies in Texas use the "Employment-at-Will" law, it means that the employer and employee have a working arrangement where either party can terminate at any time, with or without cause and with or without notice.

I understand we should all be mindful of our choice of words. We have to be conscious of how what we say may affect people. But I began to question how a word that isn't in a real dictionary could evoke so much hostility and drama. Should we let words have that much control over us? Should people be fired for saying something by accident or using a word they don't know has racist connotations? Should people lose their job because someone's feelings were hurt, even if the hurt was not intentional? Was this a valid case of racism, or was this a case of someone simply being offended?

Being offended in the workplace can become a tricky situation. There's a fine line between a real offense and an incident that could have been resolved with a conversation mediated by the managers to clear up the misunderstanding. In this case, it was easier for the company to defuse the situation by letting go of the offender, rather than coming up with a better solution to the situation.

Anything and everything can go amuck when working with people who are not professional, especially in lower-level jobs which have less stability to begin with. I decided right then and there that I wanted to be a part of a place that cared about actual professionalism, ethics, and the well-being and job stability of its employees. I wanted to work somewhere where management would wait to talk to all the witnesses of an incident before passing judgment, and where they would try to address and resolve situations in a better way. I concluded that I would find work with people who understood what real leadership was, made considered decisions, and dealt with conflict better.

I just didn't know how long it would take to find a job that fit those criteria.

Chapter 5

Fast Cash

Welcome to adulthood! This exciting new time in your life is full of bills in your name piling up, student loans to pay back, and drinks to consume to alleviate the pressure. The hustle begins! Sometimes desperate times call for desperate measures, and you may find yourself needing some fast cash. You may even turn to gig work: an alley cat race in which finding and completing a simple task can take on frustrating dimensions. Some ways of earning a quick buck seem viable, others not so viable. Let's see what our options are... *(watch out... some jest ahead)*.

1. Work at Starbucks

Woohoo! Free coffee!!! Except "free" comes with a price, namely dealing with caffeine addicts and learning to concoct obnoxious drink orders. *Venti, half organic sugar, grass-fed non-fat milk, and extra shot of Dolce and Gabbana, with a smiley face atop the extra foam... please! Ariana Grande mocha choco latte yah yah!* Plus, if you haven't yet earned a degree, Starbucks will pay for you to attend Arizona State University online!

2. Baby-sit or pet-sit

The last thing you want to do is take care of someone else's screaming kids while following their parents' crazy rules, but you talk yourself into it because you "like kids." Let's be honest, even if you do like kids, it's not like you want to spend every day around them. But hey, you're desperate, and it pays above minimum wage in some cases. Maybe dealing with constant whining, pooping, and vomiting isn't so bad?

Or perhaps you connect better with animals. They are so cute and cuddly and—OUCH! The little bastard bit you and ran away with your cell phone in its mouth!

3. Get a part time job in retail or at a restaurant

So... you "like people," huh? Then you must have the chops for voluntary servitude! Welcome to the world of having to smile and deal with stupid people... all day long. God forbid you do anything wrong, or you will be yelled at by an entitled customer attempting to return something without a receipt or order a cocktail without an ID. Never mind you could be fired for these appeasements—you're just a robot to these people anyway. The turnover rates are high in these fields for a reason. You will dream of screaming, "I QUIT!" and storming out the door after throwing salt and pepper shakers in the air and causing a ruckus! But hmm, maybe you will meet some new friends—fellow servants—along the way.

4. Sell your stuff online

Look around. What do you own that you don't absolutely need? The kitchen table that never gets used? A dusty old Xbox 360 from college? Last year's iPhone? A signed poster of Aziz Ansari? You know those books you paid $400 to use for one semester? That should net you a cool $23 back! Ask your friends, post on Craigslist and OfferUp... and see what kind of cash you can get.

Warning: Be wary of sketchy people wanting to buy your stuff, but then suddenly find themselves in some crazy, dire situation right before your scheduled meet-up. They forgot they had a kid and left them at soccer practice for three hours! Their grandma got high off bath salts and stole the truck! Their roommate's dog broke a leg jumping off the balcony! They realize the cost to treat their pet snake was higher than expected, and they just can't afford that GPS anymore. This assumes you even hear back with a comprehendible reply. They found a better deal at "Breezy Butts." Perhaps that is the strangest auto-correction for Best Buy, ever? The world may never know.

5. Sell your plasma

Okay, so this is not a "get rich quick" option. And it's not for those who faint at the sight of needles. Selling your plasma is invasive, it pays a low rate of $20 to $50 per visit, and you can only do it up to twice a week. But you have a hot date lined up and you need money to wine and dine your new sweetheart. So just go to the clinic and camp out for an hour, sell your bodily fluids, and collect your cash. You'll then be on your merry way to dinner. You can now afford some drinks to help you forget that you gave up something of yourself, never mind that you don't even know exactly what plasma is…

6. Dress up as a character from a movie

Ever since the economy took a turn, the streets in Vegas and Orlando have been flooded with people dressed up as Disney princesses, or as characters from *The Hangover*, trying to make an extra buck. You can do this too! For only $5, tourists can take a picture with you dressed as Bumblebee, while you try not to sweat completely through your Transformers costume. It's hard to make a dollar in a decent way, so at least you will feel a little creative. And at the same time, if your costume is good enough, no one will even know who you are!

7. Sell arts and crafts

Have some creative talent? You could create art and sell it to your friends, or at the street market in between the guy selling feather cranium accessories (shed by his own pet birds), and the man playing several instruments at once. This way, everyone can see how talented (and poor) you are. You could also crochet a pouf ottoman, or build diaper cakes and sell them through Etsy. Embrace your creative side!

8. Freelance

Are you a writer, editor, translator, animator, videographer, or anything similar? Then the world of freelancing is there at the click of your mouse. Finding a good gig will be like searching for a unicorn in a world full of donkeys. But you get to be your own boss... sort of. "Please complete this deadline in 2.5 hours, over Thanksgiving, while also paying attention to this very particular laundry list of expectations. Payment will be made upon completion . . . within 90 days."

You may feel isolated and distracted at times, slowly becoming a professional procrastinator. Because taking time to find all the missing socks the laundry monster mysteriously ate suddenly seems important when you are on a deadline. You may begin to wonder if all this angst will lead to drinking too much vodka. Aw, screw it... alcohol helps you get creative, right?

9. Find odd jobs on Craigslist

Craigslist is a useful tool for finding random jobs when you need a quick buck. A crazy person is always willing to pay another crazy person do some oddball task. Oh, look here: an opportunity to smell people's stinky breath to evaluate the effectiveness of mouthwash! Hope you don't pass out! Here's one to be a foot model! Could be time to finally shave your feet. Here's one to be a Feline Lap Surrogate for $15 an hour! Kitty just wants a lap to cuddle on!

How about being a human guinea pig? The local clinic is paying $200 for you to test new skin cream. What could possibly go wrong? Worst-case scenario, you get a bad case of the itchies, or the product turns your skin green. It's not like you have to be in public that often. Best-case scenario, you have no side effects… and you get to pay your student loan for the month. Yay!

10. Drive for Uber or Lyft

Stalking airports, concert venues and bars will be your new forte! You also will gain experience learning the art of "small talk" or "data mining" for personal stories or information to include in that freelance blog post you were contracted to write. Take time out of your own party nights to take drunkards safely home, and hope that they don't throw up all over your clean car or try to become your new best friend. People with road rage need not apply.

11. Open a(nother) credit card

Ohhhhhh... this is the life. You can buy whatever you want with zero percent interest for six months, plus reward points! It's not real money yet, right?

12. Become an Airbnb host

Are your parents out of town? Do you have a friend's couch you can crash on? Do you enjoy having strangers in your home? Market your family home as a "quaint bed and breakfast" to travelers and make a couple hundred bucks. You don't even have to worry about health codes and regulations! Although, you might be left with a trashed house... or a squatter...

13. Join a pyramid scheme

Makeup, wrinkle cream, energy drinks, weight loss supplements, jewelry, ugly leggings, and more... You have your pick of options! All you have to do is invest $500 in ten cases of Miracle Gold, find room to store it all, and then try to sell it to all your other poor friends. They will grow tired of your Facebook invites to "events" and your annoying sales pitches that flood their social media sites. Oh, but you will get 33.333% off your next purchase if you can convince three other friends to join the pyramid as well!

14. Gamble

Fifty dollars on the Cowboys! Twenty-five bucks on red! Beer pong bets or *Bachelor* show brackets! Win money. Lose money. Develop your "system." Claim it works. Hope your friends don't stage an intervention.

15. Sell your sperm or eggs

Not worried about potentially creating hundreds of children without your knowledge? Well, men, you can donate your sperm for a few extra bucks. It's pretty easy to pump, peace out, and forget about it.

Donating eggs is a totally different story. It's not like women can pop out eggs like chickens. If you qualify, after passing all the marks on the long checklist the doctors give you, you could earn upwards of $10,000, depending on the company and the demand for your genetics. You look to be a smart cookie, so someone should appreciate a mini version of you! It's a serious deal, though, going to doctor's appointments, giving yourself shots, and going through surgery. If you're really dedicated, you can become a surrogate mother and carry someone else's baby to term. Added bonus: it's a great excuse to eat for two!

16. Become an escort or a stripper

If you don't mind exploiting your body to the fullest degree, then this might be the perfect gig for you! Who doesn't enjoy being someone's arm candy—and maybe a bit more—for a few extra bucks? If you can't seem to find work as an escort, there's also the local strip club that's always hiring. Or, mine for gold online. Sites that connect sugar daddies or mommas with sugar babies have shown a rapid increase in popularity among college students and young adults, so make sure you have some good "head shots."

17. Sell drugs

Make some easy cash as the friendly neighborhood "pharmacist." If Nancy Botwin can do it, so can you—right, dude? Your "clients" may need their fix at all hours of the night, so be prepared! You could imagine growing your business into an empire! You could imagine yourself wearing gold chains and swimming in gold coins like Scrooge McDuck! Who cares if the cops are closer than you think? You'll be one cool cat. Dolla Dolla bills, y'all!

18. Become a hobo

When all else fails and your life has completely fallen apart—your art didn't sell, you've donated as much of your body as you can for the month, and you've "sampled" all the drugs you were supposed to sell—the vagrant life might be your last option. Ah yes, the simple life. You don't have to worry about rent, nice clothes, or showering. You might already be living on your friend's couch anyway. All you need is a blanket, some food, and a swig of Sailor Jerry. Head out to a busy intersection and hold up your sign that says, "Hungry, Hungry Hobo" or "Will Twerk For Food." The laws of the universe guarantee you will score a few dollars, or at least someone's completed "free sandwich" punch card.

Along the way of trying to find myself, I dug down deep, channeled my entrepreneurial spirit, and attempted many creative and weird ways of making money. You could call me "Craigslist Kristin" like the movie *Craigslist Joe*. Many have a misconception that unemployed people are lazy or unmotivated. Well, I can tell you that I did whatever I could to make the money needed to pay my bills. I have never missed a payment on my student loans or a car payment, even when times were tough and I had no steady income. In today's day and age, it's easy to find ways to make fast cash, but I discovered that many of these may not turn out to be exactly what you signed up for.

Among the first on my list of odd jobs was participating in a marketing research study. On Craigslist, I found a center in Dallas that was looking to analyze people's brain activity while watching certain advertising campaigns. I was told to show up wearing no makeup on my eyes and nothing in my hair. *No eye makeup!?* I have invisible eyelashes, and I feel like a naked mole rat with no mascara. But I could not afford to be vain. I needed the extra $60 they were going to pay me for an hour of my time.

I showed my ID, filled out some paperwork, and was led back to a room full of elevated swivel chairs where they would prep me for the study. A woman in a white coat and glasses sat me down in one of the chairs and proceeded to put blobs of an unidentified white goop in my hair. It was so disgusting! All I could think about was how I was going to get it all out of my hair later. I looked over at another young woman also being prepped, and she seemed to be having the same thought. Then, the lab tech started sticking countless wired sensors onto different parts of my scalp. After they were satisfied with my un-washed alien look, I was taken to a small glass room, where I was to watch an ad for Tostitos and answer various questions by pressing buttons. I had to respond to colors, images, words and phrases. The process almost made me fall asleep. *I wonder if their fancy machines picked up on that fact?*

An hour later, I was done. I went to the bathroom to look at myself. I settled on the fact that I had no choice but to walk out in public looking like a monkey had done ungodly things to my hair. I brushed it as best I could, and went to collect my $60 check. This was around the same time I got my tax return from the government. I paid my loan, bought lunch… and bought a pair of shoes. *Hey, don't judge, they were for interviews!*

Thank you, Tostitos. Not only are you delicious, but you aided in funding another one of my addictions (shoes). I wonder if they were secretly hoping that whatever they had done to my brain would convince me to blow my money on chips and salsa? *Not happening, Tostitos. Not happening.*

One of my first sketchy experiences with Craigslist was getting hired for a day to sell breast cancer T-shirts for charity at my Alma Mater during homecoming. I met up with a bunch of other young ladies in a local hotel lobby where we were told to walk around collecting $20 cash for each shirt; whoever sold the most would get a bonus. When I was hired I thought it was legit, but as the day went on I started to feel that we were just ripping off my fellow fans!

As I wandered the campus with another girl who had countless tattoos, we were approached by a Director at the school who asked if we were an approved vendor. When we couldn't answer the question, that's when the spark lit. I knew it was not right. This so called "marketing for charity" was a scam company, traveling the country and getting naive girls to collect as much money as possible from college game goers. They weren't actually associated with a charity, and were just making a profit on the T-shirts. People were willing to buy the shirts, so I had been collecting a lot of money from people who thought they were supporting a good cause.

Since I was fresh out of school, one of my old roomies still lived on campus, so I was able to hitch a ride back to the hotel where my car was. My heart grew heavy, knowing that this company wasn't real. This dishonest scheme wasn't the way to get the cash I needed. I got back to the hotel, and left the shirts and money behind. I did not feel right taking all the dirty money, even if I desperately needed it.

Another way I was able to get some quick cash was working for Edible Arrangements during the Mother's Day holiday. I was hired on the spot because of my *charming* personality. It was eight days' worth of work, and paid $7.75 an hour. This company always has to hire temps during busy holiday times. People love their fruit baskets! I learned quickly how to take orders on the phone and process them through the company's system. It was ridiculous recommending $75 baskets of overpriced fruit to people. The markups on these things were crazy! On the plus side, I now know how to fashion my own arrangements at home, and I got to eat unlimited strawberries and pineapple for a week. Thank you for not letting me starve that week, Edible Arrangements!

One summer I was searching in the writing gigs section of Craigslist trying to find a way to cover some bills. I found a man who was starting his own affordable fashion website and needed someone to write product descriptions. I warily drove out to his warehouse on Harry Hines Blvd. For those of you who don't know Dallas, this is an area that can be quite sketchy and is home to drug dealers and hookers who hang out under bridges.

I met up with an Indian man who called himself Patel. He was probably around 32 at the time, attractive and well dressed. He walked me into his fairly empty warehouse, where he showed me his purses, scarves, watches, bracelets and a bunch of other random accessories scattered about. There was a table set up in the middle of the warehouse where a photographer was taking pictures of the items against a white backdrop.

Patel, who had just met me, a stranger off the Internet nonetheless, helped me load my car with around 100 purses and accessories. He wanted me to go home, name them, and write a two- to three-sentence description about each one. I spent a lot of time sitting on the floor of my room playing with the purses, trying on the accessories and modeling in front of the mirror.

A week later, when I went to return the accessories to Patel, I ran into a young woman at the warehouse who coincidently was my co-worker at another sales gig I was working at the time. She was also writing descriptions for Patel. What were the chances that both of us were working the same two temp jobs to try to make cash during these hard times? *I love coincidences!* I was paid about $200 cash for all my descriptions, and I never heard from Patel again. I later looked up his site when it went live, and found that he had not used any of my creative names or descriptions! The descriptions used were *boring!* But it didn't matter. A few years later the site shut down and it became another case of a failed start-up.

One of my more random experiences trying to make some quick cash was at a Tea Party Rally at a Minor League Baseball stadium in Dallas. I hardly knew anything about the Tea Party, much less identified at all with their political views. I was hired to sell $2 hand-held American flags to people as they came into the stadium, and I would get a certain percentage of the money. I tried to approach every single person that walked into that stadium to up my chances. I sold $100 worth of flags in hard cash in the hour before the event was set to begin. But my keep was just 20 percent. I could have just walked out and gone home with that $100, but, instead, I turned in the $80 bucks and left with $20—enough to buy some gas and some food for the day. Somewhere online, there are pictures of me looking happy, holding an American flag at a Tea Party event. Know that I was NOT happy!

You would think that after many sour experiences on Craigslist I would have become overwhelmed and just given up. But I kept on and even sold anything of value I was willing to give up like purses, jewelry, designer jeans, furniture, an iPod and GPS. I also got a kick out of browsing Craigslist for random jobs. Needless to say, my first two years out of college were funded, in part, by the most random events and people I could ever have imagined. I learned that when strapped for cash, "Craig" will be there to help me through! Just maybe not as helpful as I had hoped.

Chapter 6

Is This A Scam?

While on the job hunt in my early years after college, I applied to anything that would boost my resume in some way, because the degree I had spent five years of my life earning was not getting me very far. Every job that sounded interesting required so much previous experience; something I lacked. Because of this, many employers would not even respond to my e-mails. I felt frustrated by it all, often locking myself in my room to sulk. I was still working in retail, hoping for an opportunity with room for growth.

I eventually came across an ad that looked something like this:

MARKETING & ADVERTISING—ENTRY LEVEL OPENINGS! SUCCESS and RAPID EXPANSION— The Company is looking to fill MULTIPLE entry-level positions in marketing & advertising. Our Company lives by a philosophy of loyalty to our consumers and results for our clients. Our SUCCESS is built upon the standards of promoting from within, leading by example, and working as hard for our clients as we would for ourselves. We believe communication and development is the KEY TO SUCCESS in any industry or field. Our philosophy emphasizes the importance of learning, improving, and having a full understanding of the business model. Employees will be trained in the following:

- *MARKETING & ADVERTISING*
- *ACCOUNT MANAGEMENT*
- *PROMOTIONAL SALES*
- *LEAD GENERATION*
- *DEMOGRAPHIC RESEARCH*
- *TEAM MANAGEMENT*

Sounds promising enough, *right?* I applied for the job and, astonishingly, heard from them the very next day! After a general phone screening with a cheerful young woman, I was then invited to an in-person interview. I was excited and blinded by optimism. *It sure was easy to get that initial interview.* I couldn't wait to see what the company had to offer.

The day of my interview I drove to an office building in North Dallas that was a shared space for many small businesses. When I finally made it through the right door, I saw that it opened into a small waiting area that had two more doors on either side of the wall. I caught a glimpse of what was inside one of the doors and saw an empty room full of boxes and whiteboards clinging to the wall. There were about 15 young people all around the room, going through what I instinctively knew was a motivational sales meeting. I heard them chanting and applauding. *What did I get myself into now?* As I sat in the tiny waiting room, rubbing elbows with six other young people there for the same thing, I thought, the ad for the job must have been like catnip growing in a backyard, drawing in all the kitties within smelling distance.

I was called behind the second door and found myself in a small office where I sat in front of two people. The man and the woman, both in their late twenties, introduced themselves as the manager and assistant manager of the company branch. They asked me fairly basic interview questions, while describing how awesome it was to work for this company. They bragged and bragged. Then they told me that since they liked me, they wanted me to go to an on-site interview that day. I grabbed my purse and followed the enthusiastic woman out of the office. She said we would need to drive separately to the location site. We began the trek, which was a lot longer than I expected.

We ended up at a popular bulk buying club about 25 minutes from the main office and a whopping hour from my home. The manager told me that this job would require a lot of traveling to different club locations in the Dallas area. As we proceeded into the store, she began to tell me more details about the job. I would be an event marketing representative, much like the promo girls you see at bars. However, instead of just promoting the brand, I would push for sales right then and there. I wasn't exactly sure what the products were yet.

I was introduced to one of the gals who had been with the company for a few months, and had recently been promoted to a trainer. In casual conversation, the tall, model type said she'd gone to a popular state university. She then proceeded to demonstrate what I would be doing if I was hired. The job consisted of setting up the event booth every day and then walking around the store soliciting people to buy the "special" products that were offered for a "limited time." The shows would run two weeks at a particular location. After that, the company would rotate new products and a new team of two to three went in to work the store. Sales reps never stayed at one location selling the same thing for more than a couple of weeks.

The beautiful gal made her job look easy. She demonstrated a hand cream and a nail buffer with ease and composure. The first two people she approached and conversed with wanted the items and put the items in their cart.

"*See how easy!*" the woman interviewing me said beaming, with a big, proud smile. We then went to the food court in the store where I was able to ask more general questions about the job. The two told me the company would pay for my gas when traveling to the job sites. They told me that this was just the entry level stage and that I would have the opportunity to move up and become a team lead, training other people to do the job, then an account manager working more of the behind the scenes of the business. Eventually I could run an office of my own. With enough hard work, I could become my own boss. They stressed that the goal was to be able to open my own office anywhere in the United States. The promise of the American dream was stressed: the ideal that everyone should have an equal opportunity to achieve success and prosperity through hard work, determination, and initiative; the dream of making a better life for yourself and your offspring.

This all sounded pretty exciting to me. I liked the idea of being my own boss. They promised to pay me at least minimum wage, but the job was mostly based on a 20 percent commission, which they said would add up to good money. They said they were having a health benefits meeting soon, and we could go over my options. I was offered the job based on my "likeable personality" and was expected to start in two weeks. I was required to work weekends too, but since I already did that at the department store I worked at, it didn't seem like much of a change. It sounded like a decent opportunity, but I left that interview with an uneasy feeling. Was peddling products in a retail club really the sales and growth opportunity they made it seem like? Something about it smelled fishy, but I told myself, *we all have to start somewhere.*

After I got home, I told my boyfriend (at the time) all about the job. He encouraged me to take the position because he did not want to see me working at a clothing store anymore. He had been pressuring me to get out of working for nearly minimum wage and to bulk up my resume.

While it was technically another retail/sales job, it seemingly offered more "opportunity and room for growth." I took the plunge, quit my job, and agreed to start with the new company in two weeks. I was going to miss my old co-workers, but I knew I needed a change. Plus, everyone at the new company seemed so excited during my interview. It made me want to be excited about the job too.

When I arrived at the main office for my first morning meeting, I was greeted by about 20 other people my age, mostly female. The purpose of the early morning meetings was to learn the steps of the sales process, practice and perfect the pitch, and go over any other details needed for the day. Everyone was assigned a different product to promote. There were hair products that were supposedly used at New York Fashion week, Dead Sea skin products, "designer" makeup, a health tea designed to help you lose weight, and a car wax that was "NASCAR approved." I proceeded to learn the step-by-step sales pitch, the pyramid structure of the company, and how one could move up.

My first day in the store was tough. I was expected to talk to every single person who walked into the store. I was with one other young woman and my trainer (Ryna), all of us selling the same thing. The goal was to try to get the product into customers' hands so they would feel a sense of ownership toward the product. And the company meant it when they said *every… single… person*. Selling a hair product? You still had to talk to every old lady with a wig, bald man, and grumpy person that walked into the store. The tip I got: "Present it as a gift they can give!"

Since I am a people person, I did not have much trouble engaging strangers. Sometimes, people would stop to chat with me for a while, or occasionally buy one of the products as a gift, because I'm sure they were *ever so charmed* by my personality. Most of us doing the job would realistically get ten to twenty yes's in a day. It felt like I was told "no" about a thousand times every day. I noticed the other girls would use any possible tactic to get people to buy. I asked about where they found some of the "facts" they were telling the customers. Many just responded with, "I don't know. I heard it from someone else."

My feet often ached from standing all day and the fact that we were not provided with an actual lunch break. We had to work six to nine hours straight with no time to rest. It was killer, but since I knew it was commission-based, I didn't want to miss out on a single person who walked in the door.

A week into it, I had one of my first solo shifts for a few hours until the next girl showed up. Ryna was one of the main trainers on the hair care products that we were selling. An intimidating girl with glasses and short hair pulled tightly into a ponytail, who had an air about her that made her seem like she thought she was better than everyone else. She talked about her Master's degree in marketing all the time, and how she was on the fast track to become the next assistant manager when the current one moved on to open his own office. She wanted to open up her own store in California.

Simply put, Ryna was annoying. She got on my case about everything from tiny details about my pitch, to the sound of my voice. She even spied on me one day! She came in early and lurked in the aisles to see how I was doing. She later confronted me by saying she had seen that I didn't talk to *every single last person* who walked in the door, and that was a *no-no*. I felt a little violated! There was a certain level of trust and independence necessary to the job, and she felt like since I was new, she couldn't trust me to do my job correctly. She spied on me so she could criticize me. *Did the trainers do that to everyone?*

Despite my trainer being difficult, I pushed on, and even felt I was getting better at sales. This was a short-lived feeling. Since I had started around Christmas time, of course people were buying the products— they did make good gifts! But as time went on and the New Year began, I made fewer and fewer sales. My paychecks were not usually more than $500 (before taxes) for two weeks of work. Where was minimum wage factored into this? I realized I had not even filled out a W-4 form for this job. I was doing contract work without the legalities. I tried to ask about this, but I was never given a straight answer about how my paychecks were actually determined. I was told it would be at least minimum wage or commission, whichever was more. But minimum wage would have been at least $580 (before taxes) bi-weekly. Was it just 100 percent commission? I couldn't get a straight answer.

A couple of months passed. One day I showed up to work distracted, as I was stirring over a sticky situation involving my sister and the repercussions of it all.[vii] I approached a lady about the hair product I was selling, and she

---

[vii] More on this in Chapter 17.

listened to me talk for a minute. Then she said, "Honey, I don't really have time for this. My son died recently... and I just can't."

I became overwhelmed with sadness, and slinked away. I wasn't quite sure how to handle the situation. My crazy trainer witnessed this encounter and had the audacity to tell me that the reason the lady felt the need to tell me that her son had died was because I looked "sad and depressed" myself that day. If I had "smiled more," maybe I would have made that sale. I couldn't take her catty remarks. I ran out of the store to take a moment to breathe. How could she say something so callous? That was not positive motivation; I just did not want to deal with her anymore.

Ryna finally came outside, apologized, and asked me if I wanted to go home. Well, I wasn't going to give her the satisfaction of defeating me, so I proceeded to work the rest of the day. In fact, I worked harder than ever! That week, Ryna and I beat the record for sales for that hair product. It felt great! The club manager came up to me and said he couldn't wait to have us there again because we had boosted the store's sales. He even showed me the numbers. We had done more than $5,000 in sales in three days, which meant I was going to get a great paycheck!

When I received my paycheck for that week, it wasn't anywhere near as big as I expected. It was then I learned I only received half of the 20 percent commission. No one had told me that if you shared a shift with someone, you had to split the commission. That's when I realized that I was being ripped off. I suddenly realized I had never seen a pay stub or a breakdown of commissions. Feeling lost and confused, my mind drifted to thought of being at my old job. I even called my previous manager and asked for my department store job back, but he didn't have an opening. I didn't want to just quit, because I knew what it was like to be unemployed, and it hadn't exactly been easy to find a decent job.

The following week I was transferred to another store location and learned how to sell a new product: car wax. You would not believe the comments or cat-calls that come out of some people's mouths when they see a pretty girl selling wax. Euphemisms for the status of my lady parts were often uttered. I increasingly felt beat down by the job. I often worked shifts right before a red-headed young woman, who was so obsessed with becoming a manager that she, too, got on my case when she would see the amount of unsold product. She kept asking me about my goals with the company and where I saw myself in one year. I had to explain to her that my goals were not with this company, and that I had other aspirations. She replied, "I just couldn't take being told no every day in person for so long if I didn't have a manager position ahead of me. I would hate myself. It wouldn't be worth it." I just starred at her in silence. It gave me a lot to think about.

The turnover rate in any sales job is high. Every day I walked into that office more people had quit and new people were there to take their places. Each morning, someone would read a motivational story and try to boost the group's confidence to go into the day with a positive attitude. Our brains were also constantly being filled with the promise of opening our own businesses wherever we wanted, being in charge of others, making thousands and thousands of dollars, and supporting ourselves.

One morning the chipper office manager tried a unique way to get us motivated. She made each of us go up to the front of the room and write down our daily, monthly, and yearly goals on the white board. As each person went to the front of the room, they would start out with their daily goal being a certain number of sales or people to engage with. The common monthly goals were to move up to trainer or produce a certain commission. The yearly goal for every single person in that room was to open up their own office and become a leader to other people doing the job that we were currently doing. There was no variation. I couldn't help but feel that the constant indoctrination of *sell, sell, sell* to guarantee our own office and a $50,000[viii] a year paycheck had brainwashed many of us. I feared most were just saying what they thought the managers wanted to hear.

When my turn came, I didn't present my daily, monthly and yearly end goals as the others did. My goals did not involve moving up through the company. My goals were not to open up another office and subject other people to the unstable job I was experiencing. My goals were not to be surrounded by sketchy products all the time. Instead, my goals were to learn everything I could about sales and everything else I could learn from the people I worked with to gain experience, and to move on to find a more suitable job using my degree. The office manager didn't give me

---

[viii] Which I have since learned is not much with all of today's expenses!

a happy "Good job!" or "Good goals!" like she gave the rest. She simply gave me a halfhearted smile.

The only reason we were all working this sales job was the promise of making money, becoming a business owner, and so much more than was actually possible, given the reality of the situation. This type of company feeds on the fact that young, educated people today are so desperate to find a job that they are willing to work for little to no pay to gain experience. They focus on our desire for financial stability and independence, as all of my co-workers' goals revealed. But I had not fallen for the scheme. I never was one to follow the crowd or popular opinion. Now, free from the spell of unfulfillable promises, I tried to continue working there, but the redheaded girl was right. I couldn't take being told no every day when there was no chance for growth.

One day I went home and did a deep dive search for information on the company online. What I found shocked me. The company I worked for had changed their name and location over five times! An absurd number of college-educated young adults who had worked for the company complained about how they had fallen for a soliciting scheme. I learned that scam jobs like this exist in cities all across the United States. The companies overwhelm job boards with promises of opportunities and money and the "American Dream." They change their company names often, to avoid being found on sites like Ripoffreport.com. Employees *do* learn legitimate sales pitches and practices, but, for the most part, these companies are just get-rich-quick schemes for their owners.

The signs that this company was not legit were all there, and I felt stupid for not noticing. The morning meetings were basically brainwashing sessions to get us to believe in their business tactics, drilling into our heads that our only goal should be to work hard enough to own our own branch. I found out that the morning meetings were unpaid. Our required weekend phone preparation meetings were also unpaid. Why had I not questioned that I had never seen a pay stub? I had dipped into my savings just to get by while doing this job. I wasn't making enough money to cover my bills because I never got the amount of money I was promised, even though I ranked at the top of the sales charts many times. I barely made enough money to pay for gas. No gas money was ever given to us, nor a form for reimbursement, or advice on how to track miles for tax purposes. No one ever talked about these issues, or about how much they made, or about the fact that promises were not being fulfilled. Were some people actually "brainwashed?" When I finally did ask questions about sales and numbers, I was pulled aside by the manager and advised not to rehash crummy days with other co-workers so that they could just move on... *like a good minion does.*

It took me a couple of months to see the unfortunate paycheck pattern. I finally figured out how I was actually paid, which as I reflect, shows just how naive all my young coworkers and I were. Employees should always know exactly how they are paid, and see corresponding earning statements to verify this information. Managers should always be open and honest about how pay is determined. As it turns out, pay was all commission-based, with no safety net, meaning no real minimum wage. They had also made it sound like the job provided health insurance, but that was not actually the case. They just set employees up with an insurance agent. They hadn't told me that I would be expected to work six days a week if I didn't meet my goals. And by "my goals", I mean the amount that the company owners needed to bankroll their expensive habits. They lured us in with promises of financial freedom, management positions, moving to the city of our choice, and prizes like VIP game tickets, an evening on a yacht, or even a pair of Christian Louboutin shoes. It all sounded too good to be true, because it was! I never found out if the winners of the prizes actually received anything. People tend to work harder when there are opportunities to advance or promises of prizes or money to be made, and the company took full advantage of that aspect of human nature.

Scams like this happen every day. Shouldn't job boards be monitored to help prevent young people from falling into these schemes? I guess that is wishful thinking, since even the news isn't monitored well for fake stories. My biggest regret was that I hadn't done more extensive digging or research on this type of company before I left my department store job where at least I made ten bucks an hour (plus bonuses for opening credit card accounts) and had company-provided health insurance.

Some people might argue operations like the one I've described aren't truly scams, but that's true only if you define a scam as a situation where someone takes your money and doesn't give you what you expected in return. However, these companies do present employees with a false sense of hope, which feels sleazy. The only way you could ever succeed at running one of these businesses is if you are willing to swindle other people over and over again into pushing dumb products for you and then have no remorse for practically lying to them. These jobs are not what they're advertised to be. In my online searches, I found that most managers who went on to open their own business ended up failing, because the business model was too unstable.

After I found the Ripoff Reports on the company, I became overwhelmed with emotions. It was like when I found out a strawberry isn't really a berry, but a banana is! I felt confused and tricked. My dominant feeling was anger. I visualized jumping up and down on the managers' cars, banging my clenched fists against my chest and howling like an upset gorilla. I wanted to confront the managers about their promises, which they knew would not be kept. I wanted to print out the reports, post them on my co-workers' cars, and expose the truth. I wanted to point out that the website for the company never actually stated the company name, and that there was no "About Us" page. I wanted to point out all the lies I had been told about pay, and the money that had been withheld from me.

But I never did any of it. I was too afraid of stirring up trouble at the time. On the day when my mind and body couldn't take it anymore, I walked out two hours before my shift was supposed to end and I never looked back. I shuffled into the daylight, and the warmth of the sun felt brand new. I kept repeating in my head, "*The dog days are over... The dog days are over... The cat days are here again.*" It's nearly impossible to keep at something when nothing is worth staying for. I knew what lay ahead of me would be a tough and winding road, but it was better than the horrible pit I got in my stomach every time I showed up at that job.

Even after I had experienced and quit that disastrous job, at one point, I was so desperate for money while unemployed that I applied and got offered a job at a similar company with an eerily similar job description. My plan was do work for a week or two to earn some quick money. That, in itself, reveals just how much I needed cash; that I would submit myself to another week of pushing questionable products. The journalist in me was also curious to see just how comparable the tactics and strategies were to my previous job. Turns out, it was the same hiring process and the exact same empty promises. It was the same morning meetings that make you think you're special and that you are capable of moving up quickly to be your own boss. It left me thinking, *who came up with this business model?*

This time, I would be selling tickets to sporting events, soliciting door-to-door at businesses, restaurants, and any other place that you could just walk right in. The idea was to approach anyone you could, try to sell those tickets on the spot, collect the money, and go. *As if that doesn't sound fishy and illegal...*

My trainer at this job was a petite girl who was so determined to sell that she just walked into places that we obviously were not supposed to be. She followed legit workers into off-limit floors or card-access-only offices. The "tickets" we sold were actually a mini booklet of coupons priced at $20. You had to trade in a coupon at the box office for real tickets. Sure, you could end up getting tickets that was priced in the hundred dollar range, but the coupons came with so many restrictions in fine print, that you would most likely end up in the nosebleeds.

During the five days I worked for this company, I went into all sorts of businesses and was even dropped off in industrial areas. I often would be left behind. One time, at the end of my shift, I was stuck at a bank, miles away from my car. My trainer, who had dropped me off to canvas for a little bit on my own, was not answering my calls. I waited for an hour, alone, feeling like a scaredy-cat and contemplated calling a taxi (this was pre-Uber). I finally got a call from another number asking where I was, and the voice said she was on the way to pick me up. Apparently, my trainer's phone had died. Another day, I was dropped off in an industrial area with a couple of other ladies. At one point we became separated, and I just sat, waiting underneath a large tree in front of an office, chilling with the pink flamingos in the yard. After five days of work, I had made $250, which was less than minimum wage. I picked up my paycheck on the following Monday and never went back.

Was there a point to any of these experiences? I learned that you must research a company thoroughly, read reviews, and ask in-depth questions in interviews—like what the turnover rate is, or how long they have been in business. Make sure you know what's legal and what's not. Know what kind of paperwork you should be filling out if you are a full-time employee versus contract worker. Ask for pay stubs or proof of sales documentation. Communicate with your fellow co-workers. Know that it's okay to question certain business practices.

One of my best friends, Alec, had an unexpected positive outcome from working for a scammy company. The company he worked for had the same business model I had encountered. Its initiative was to sell "big retail" home services door to door in residential areas. This in itself should have been a sign: Any time you have to go knocking on people's doors to sell something, it should raise a red flag. Alec had to wear a suit and tie in the Texas heat, but at least was allowed to wear sneakers. I remember him being exhausted every day. He was clearly not happy with his life. But, like me and many others in the same situation, he needed a job. He was determined to show his parents that his private college education was not a waste.

One hot summer day, sweating through his suit, he dragged his feet along the pavement, knocking on doors in his assigned territory. Alec came to a house where a pretty young woman answered. He started his pitch, but she proceeded to tell him, as many did, that she was not interested in his services. He said politely that he understood, and left to go on to the next house. A few minutes later, the young woman ran outside and stated that she was not interested in what he was selling, but she was definitely interested in his phone number because she thought he was cute.

When he told me his new potential girlfriend was coming to his Fourth of July party, I joked with him that if she brought cookies, she was a keeper. I felt like a fortune cookie teller, because sure enough, she showed up with homemade red, white, and blue sugar cookies and chocolate chip cookies.

They proceeded to date for a few years while they both went through their own struggles, getting laid off from jobs, living with his parents, working odd jobs, and trying to get by… together. And indeed, they did! After years of dating, they went on to buy a house together, get married and have a baby! Not many people can say that the love of their life literally came knocking at their door.

Twists and turns and learning from mistakes are all part of the journey. Even after all these crazy, terrible jobs, I learned you can discover a lot about yourself and others while trying to navigate through the job jungle.

Gaining experience, street smarts, better judgment, wisdom and even relationships can come from wayward situations. Plus, this type of work prepares you for the realities of how you need to knock on a lot of doors to make any sort of change in your life and in society.

But even so, I still couldn't shake the feeling that post-college life had not panned out how I had hoped it would. I knew "paying my dues" was required, but it seemed like I might had overpaid.

Chapter 7

The Disconnects

If you work hard in college, you may feel that because of that work you are supposed to be set up to succeed; that people will value the fact that you were able to get that degree. Then the reality of life sets in and you realize that you, and millions of others, must continue to work at overcoming the hurdles set in place by society and the economy. You must figure out how to take what you learned in college and transform it into hirable skills.

Everyone knows that you don't learn everything in school to prepare you for the real world. That would be impossible. Many undergraduate students don't understand the connection between classroom learning and post-graduation success. Many become disgruntled, unmotivated and cynical in our struggle in the transition from school to work. While college was first created to focus on theoretic thinking, the fast paced world now expects you to know so much more. Employers increasingly value skills that often aren't taught on the average college campus. And most students are completely unaware of employer demands because we are so focused on grades and the curriculum set before us.

Real-world application:

After college, I often wondered why there was such a disconnect between the actualities of the workplace versus most of what I learned in school. I often felt I left college without learning the hands-on tools it would take to land an actual job, such as program management or specific technical abilities traditionally learned through practitioner work. These are problems that many young adults are facing across all majors: too much theory and not enough hands-on learning. Are colleges constantly evaluating their curriculum and changing it to align with the need of industry and society? We rely on the colleges to know what is best for us. I suspect the majority of colleges are still trying to catch up with the ever changing workplace requirements. College students in every field also need to learn the hard skills that are used in the workplace.

I was in the communications school and took many classes on writing, theory, and presenting, but post-college I often wondered why I did I not learn relevant software and technology needed to land a job. For example, why did I not learn content management systems, photo and video editing, Google Analytics, WordPress or other relevant media and communication software? Why were these not part of the curriculum, yet employers expect most communications major applicants to know the fundamentals of these type of software and programs? Basic Microsoft Suite is not enough. Why wasn't I at least advised to learn these types of programs? When else would I learn these programs, if not in college, where I am paying thousands of dollars to get a well-rounded education? It's not like employers are investing money in training graduates to learn these programs...[ix] *Is this the type of stuff you must teach yourself by watching YouTube?*

On top of learning relevant technology, we need to learn soft skills that translate to the workplace. Employers say that some top skills they are looking for is teamwork, collaboration, and the ability to think on your feet. According a PayScale survey, 60% of managers claim the new graduates they see taking jobs within their organizations do not have the critical thinking and problem solving skills they feel are necessary for the job.[16]

The best classes I took in college were the ones in which the professors made us engage with other students, working on a large topical project that required multiple aspects of applied learning outside of the classroom. In a sustainability class during my senior year, I was put into a group of five to do a project on some aspect of being "green." Our assignment: "Eliminating Paper Waste on Campus." As a group, we had to write a ten-page paper on how we would implement the idea in the real world, create a commercial video on the subject, create a poster to represent our ideas, and present our research and argument at a campus event for sustainability.

[ix] More on this in Chapter 16.

The winner would receive a prize and be mentioned in the University's newspaper and PR outlets.

My group included people from all different backgrounds. We decided to split up the work based on our strengths and then come together as a whole to discuss, edit, and prepare our final project. We communicated well and were able to work around each other's crazy schedules so that we could meet at the library for brainstorming sessions. We turned ideas into ways to really change the campus. By gathering our strengths and working on a project that had real effects outside the classroom, and competing in a competition, we learned valuable skills that could be taken outside the classroom.

We all need to learn teamwork and collaboration and how to work with different kinds of people. We need to learn adaptability and how to make changes when a hitch comes up in a project. We need to learn confidence by actually seeing a project through from start to finish. We need to learn leadership skills and how to direct a group to successful outcomes. We need to learn a healthy sense of competition and how to be innovative to stand above the rest. These are the tools needed to be successful in the real world. These are skills that make a person hirable. Schools would do well to focus classes on these types of applied learning, instead of focusing on mostly on standardized tests and lecture based classes.

While many schools are aware of how to implement these types of learning, a problem that many graduates struggle with is how to translate aptitude onto paper to showcase these learned soft skills on resumes, cover letters and interviews. Figuring out how to match your skills can feel about as discombobulating as having your Internet disconnected. You feel lost, but you have to remember that the computer still works. You're plenty capable; you may just have to adjust your settings. College Career Centers should be helping students find these connections when writing resumes and cover letters. Giving specific examples and hard numbers are always a helpful way to explain your capabilities.

To survive, schools must not only address their internal cost structures, they must also take a hard look at the relevance and delivery of their courses. Many colleges need to fix the curricula that will help students find good work or qualify for advancement, and deliver it in a manner that accommodates the way students want and need to learn. Educators should prove to students that the education we are getting will be worth the money, making it more likely that if we put the hard work in, we will graduate and be set up for a good job. College should be preparing students for entry into the real world. It's not like college is a trip to Vegas. What happens in college can't just stay in college.

The internship dilemma:

The whole point of internships is to get real world experience, enhance your resume, gain interesting knowledge and take advantage of networking opportunities. For some, an internship can lead to a job offer. We should embrace every opportunity we can to learn from professionals. The problem is, only so many good internships exist, and with so many people competing for them, many students are willing to work for no pay just to get a paw in the door.

The U.S. Department of Labor guidelines state that internships must be to the benefit of the intern. If the internship provides an opportunity to refine what students are learning in school, to learn to do real-world tasks, or to shadow an expert, that internship exists for the benefit of the intern. These interns stand to learn what is not typically taught in school, and these types of internships ultimately provide value.

The guidelines also say that unpaid internships should *only* be acceptable if the student gains more from the experience than the intern sponsor receives in labor. If the intern is doing anything that helps the company profit or is doing work someone else is getting paid for, the intern should be paid. If a student is working at the internship, as opposed to only observing or shadowing, then it can be argued one should get paid at least a fair wage. Unpaid internships can lead to inequality in the workplace, and might even devalue the job itself; if a company can get an unpaid or low-paid intern to do entry-level work, that takes away an entry-level job from someone who needs—and deserves—to be paid.

But organizations that attract enough qualified applicants for their internships can afford to not only be extremely picky about whom they hire, but can also use these interns with impunity. Many organizations simply take on college interns to get more help with menial tasks around the office. You know, like fetching coffee, sorting packets of sugar or walking the boss's Pekingese. These interns aren't actually learning anything, and these "jobs" could potentially be considered illegal per the Department of Labor. *Might as well be working at Starbucks over the summer instead, because at least a paycheck would be involved!* But students are determined to do all they can to stand out from the crowd, which includes agreeing to work for free or accepting the crazy idea that just making coffee and copies is a worthwhile use of time.

For broke college students, sometimes taking an unpaid internship is simply not an option. This perpetuates the already existing inequality in our society between those who come from families who can afford to pay for college and living expenses and those who don't have any help. And an unsettling fact that is often left out of the unpaid internship debate is that many students have to pay their college for the credits earned through an internship, just as one would pay for all other credits earned from classes... even if one works for free.

When I interned for the news station CBS 11, I had the opportunity to ride around with reporters and videographers, and be on the scene when something was going down. I saw a variety of stories unfold before me, including the police busting a house with a secret underground marijuana business, a dead body pulled from a river, the reaction to a bomb threat at a mall... I even went to a birthday party for a 106-year-old woman.[x] The internship was a great way to see inside the news world, but the big lesson

---

[x] She told me the secret to a long life is to surround yourself with good people.

it taught me was that being a news reporter wasn't exactly what I wanted to do every day for the rest of my life. However, I was already four years into school, so there was no turning back on my major.

I had to pay my university more than $2,000 to get the credit for the "internship class." The internship was three days a week, unpaid. I was driving back and forth from Fort Worth to Dallas (about an hour drive between the two cities) to balance a job that paid, with the internship that didn't. The problem was that the school did absolutely nothing to prepare me for the internship. I had applied and done everything to get the internship on my own. My college never told me what was required of me as a student while at my internship. I received no e-mails, no forms and no syllabus. The only things I received were a bill and an 'I' for "incomplete" at the end of the summer. No one told me there were certain forms I needed to have filled out by my internship supervisor, or certain criteria the internship had to meet. I ended up going through a strenuous process to prove I had done the internship in order to get my 'I' turned into an 'A'.

If having an internship is a requirement for graduation, as it should be, should students be paying for the credits if the school doesn't have anything to do with providing or securing the internship? It seems suspiciously like a way for colleges to make some easy money. Shouldn't schools be more proactive about helping students gain real-world experiences, especially if they are going to charge for the credit?

Decisions, decisions:

As I looked deeper into how American colleges are not exactly preparing students for the real world, I realized that the issues start before students ever reach college. I began to question the whole concept of deciding what we want to be when we "grow up" during our senior year of high school. I don't know about you, but when I was 17, I was more involved with my extracurricular activities, getting my driver's license, and surviving high school drama, than in choosing a major that could decide what I would do for the rest of my life. Of course I was concerned with my future, and had always had a healthy anxiety about where I was going and how I would get there, but the decision of what I wanted to do with the rest of my life felt rushed. Sure, some seniors in high school are mature enough and confident enough to know how to make the right choices, but many are picking something—whether it's a college, a major, or a vocation—just because we are told to do so. Hell, many people in all stages of life still don't know what we were put on this earth to do.

For teenagers nearing the end of high school, the pressure is on. Parents, teachers, and older siblings keep saying the same comments: *"Figure it out! Devise a plan! Design your life! Don't waste your youth!"* But figuring out an end game is extremely difficult, especially if you don't even know where the starting line is drawn. Ultimately, no one is perfectly prepared for what happens once the bubble of school bursts and you are left to figure out next steps. No more set standard tells you how much studying will equate to a higher grade in life. No amount of time at the library will set you up for what is to come. Reality hits, and many graduates are left scared or overwhelmed. It's like being thrown into a pool for the first time, without any floaties.

Re-vamping secondary education:

While colleges need to assess how they are preparing students for the real world, we also need to assess how high schools are preparing students for both college and adult life in general. Are there enough opportunities available for average students to find a purpose before launching into the real world? Experts agree that making changes to high school education should be a priority.[17] While I do not claim to be an authority in education reform, I have experienced disconnects between the real world and education, and have complied my thoughts in alignment with what some experts think we can do. I do know that certain changes to programs or curriculums could help students and young adults navigate the real world a bit easier. We cannot change education overnight. But we can begin to formulate teaching and interactions around entrepreneurship, work/study programs, internships, apprenticeships, and education in the skills and programs hiring employers are actually looking for. We need a good balance between critical thinking, job and life training, and creative outlets, like art and music.

It may come as shock, but many high schools are not even teaching valuable life skills. Many people are leaving school without the slightest idea about what it takes to manage daily life![xi] Students should learn how to write a resume, how to set a budget, how to follow the stock market, what a 401k is, how insurance works, and how to lead a healthy lifestyle. *Eat your vegetables, kids!* Students should also be taught, at bare minimum, the ins and outs of basic laws that might affect their regular lives. Additionally, supplements for what to do outside the classroom should be made available to students so it's known it takes more than just passing classes to be set up for a career.

With constant changes in technology, social norms, and job descriptions, we need to change how we prepare the young to become contributing members of society. STEM (science, technology, engineering, and mathematics) jobs go unfilled because kids lose interest in math and science. Kids have been asking for years in math and science classes, "How will I use this in the real world?" We can't just teach math equations to memorize for an upcoming test. Kids want to know how and why things work and why it's important to the world. Kids want to know how what is being taught can create a better future. Students don't want to know just how to solve math problems, but how math can solve our problems too.[xii] But the same goes for all subjects; students need to understand how what

---

[xi] Of course, parents should be instilling this information as well!

[xii] The blonde claimed, *"But I'm not good at math! You know subjects like... um... geo...graphs? And calcu...lators."* ;-)

is being taught applies to the real world. Schools must introduce new ways of teaching that show kids how what they are learning can be implemented.

Closer collaboration between policymakers, educators, and businesses, and the ever growing changing and technology scene is needed to help align young people's skills with business needs. Encouraging partnerships between high schools and private industries is important. We need to expand existing programs that help students receive specialized job training in high-demand fields, such as manufacturing, information technology, or health care, all while working toward a high school degree and earning college credits. Schools could shift their focus from test scores and graduation rates to increasing project-based learning and placing students in more internships. This would allow some people to become empowered to choose between universities, other job paths, or to just be more creative in life choices.

Schools should create more registered apprenticeship programs to give students hands-on training in marketable skills in conjunction with regular classroom instruction. Apprenticeships can help develop those skills in fields such as engineering, health care, or carpentry, while also giving many young people a first time work experience. Working with a mentor in high school and college, whether it is someone in the industry or someone in retirement looking to make changes to young people's lives, will increase student interest. When people have a connection in a field of interest, someone to talk to and learn from, deciding a future can feel less daunting and more understandable.

Programs such as SPARK!, which launched in 2004, helps 7th, 8th, and 9th graders get set up with mentors to help them succeed in their coming of age years when it is super important to keep students engaged. By liaising working professionals and connecting businesses with local communities, according to SPARK's web-site, the program empowers the next generation to perform better in school, graduate on time and lead fulfilling careers and lives.

Education also needs to be more globally focused. In our increasingly interconnected world there's no excuse for students and schools to live in a bubble. Global learning curriculums can help students begin a journey of feeling more open minded, compassionate, connected and curious about others. Students should be learning about human cultures, the physical and natural world, basic concepts and new developments in science and technology, global socio-political issues, and our implications for the future and the role of America in the world. This will help students start thinking about how to make a difference in this world that is facing major problems like climate change and an unstable global political landscape.

A heavy focus on multiple choice tests and standardized tests in America does little to advance real-world goals such as college readiness and career preparation. A 2011 National Research Council report said: "Despite using them for several decades, policymakers and educators do not yet know how to use test-based incentives to consistently generate positive effects on achievement and to improve education."[18] After No Child Left Behind passed in 2002, the US dropped from 18th in the world in math on the Programme for International Student Assessment (PISA) to 31st place in 2009, with a similar drop in science and no change in reading.[19] Students now days are also spending much time stressing and studying for tests that drop them in a box, instead of thinking outside of it.

Even those at the top of high school classes are often ill-prepared for college. A 2008 report by the education advocacy group Strong American Schools found that 80 percent of college students who had to take remedial classes had a high school GPA of 3.0 or better.[20] While often frustrating for professors who are forced to spend a semester teaching concepts their students should have learned by the end of 12th grade, remedial classes also come with more serious consequences. Students are likely to drop out of college if it seems like college is just like repeating high school. The value of a college education is only as good as the ability to gain new skills, instead of relearning old ones.

Taxpayers also suffer by "paying twice" for students to take high-school-level classes again, since most remedial work doesn't count toward college graduation. In the 2007-08 academic year, remedial courses cost about $5.6 billion. $3.6 billion in "direct educational costs," such as taxpayer contributions to state universities, and another $2 billion in "lost wages"—a result of giving up on higher education and missing out on the higher paychecks that can come with college degrees.[21]

Community college is a relatively affordable way to try out college and see if it's the right path. But to avoid community college becoming the new high school, we need to raise expectations—and reading levels—during high school. Students must possess competencies in math, reading, and writing before entering college; community colleges should not be required to fulfill this role. While we can't wave a magic wand to improve this instantly, we need to stop expecting students to successfully go to college with eighth-grade math and reading skills. Habits of success and taking on challenges need to take root long before seniors graduate.

Budgeting change, getting people on board with new ideas, and actually implementing those innovations is never easy. I question how long it will take policy makers to understand what is happening to the youth of America and realize it is worth the time to repave the foundation on which we rely. At least in the meantime, as we notice the disconnects, we can do our best to start filling in some of the gaps by doing quality internships or apprenticeships, expanding our skill sets, and seeking out a relationship between our education and where we want it to take us.

Chapter 8

College Issues (Cost and Value)

Sarcastic College Recruiter:

Hey kids, you don't want to be flipping burgers or cleaning toilets your whole life, right? Then go to college! It's kind of like being on unemployment, but your parents are proud of you! That's of course, if you don't have to work a minimum wage gig to get through school or pay for the ridiculously priced textbooks and living quarters. Going to college will get you a degree, which will get you a better job, which will make you more money.

But we can only guarantee the degree part... if you can make it through the high-pressure stress and professors scheduling exams and presentations during the same week. You will have to take a bunch of classes for the first two years that have nothing to do with your area of study. We just want you to be well-rounded in subjects that you could probably learn by doing a simple web search.

Unless you have loaded parents, or you're the next star athlete, you will have to take out huge loans. The good news is you don't have to start paying money back until after you graduate… or drop out. Don't worry; you'll get ten to fifteen years to pay it back!

Unless you die. Then, hey, you're off the hook!

After I graduated from college, I struggled to repay my student loan debt since I could not find a reputable job. If I was having this much trouble finding decent work with a degree, was the degree and the debt that came with it worth it? I couldn't help but reflect on the cost and value of college, especially since so much about higher education has been scrutinized in the news in recent years, something that previous generations have not experienced with such full force in the past. In today's world, the reality is that a large percentage of Millennials go to college and graduate, but find it difficult to find a job related to their major, or something steady that provides enough income to meet living expenses *and also* pay back the debt taken on to get that degree.

Traditional colleges, community colleges and for-profit colleges (a newer beast) have all been called out on what they do and what they cost. It seems not all colleges are created equal. Just what has been going on in recent years in the college landscape that has affected the current generation's playing field? Why has college become so expensive? Why is it that the price of college continues to rise, yet the average pay rate has remained stagnant? Where is our money going when we pay tuition? What are we really getting out of college?

College costs have risen by 1,120 percent since 1978, far outpacing the increase in costs for other goods and services.[22] Despite the fact that more students and families struggle to pay for higher education, enrollments continue to increase. People recognize that more education leads to higher potential throughout life, so finding a way to finance education through loans becomes important.

Student debt from college loans has grown faster than any other type of individual debt (including credit cards), topping $1.3 trillion by 2016. That's $1,300,000,000,000! That is a lot of zeros! If the Federal Government were a private company, it would be the most profitable company in the world. The Congressional Budget Office projects that the Federal Government made nearly $50 BILLION on student loan interest in 2013.[23]

Student loans are unique for a number of reasons; most importantly, nothing can disqualify an applicant from a federally-backed loan, excluding a prior student loan default or a drug conviction. A student loan is quite possibly the only loan that is not tied to credit worthiness or the ability to repay. The U.S. Government can garnish wages and withhold tax-refunds to satisfy unpaid student debt. It's almost impossible to get out of paying a student loan, except in the case of death! Even more frustrating is that these easy loans are correlated to the rising cost of college tuition—colleges have every incentive to raise costs, knowing that an endless supply of money exists in the form of loans. Loans given directly to students help cushion the increase in industry costs.

The rising cost of college is not just due to how easy it is to get a loan. State college funding cuts have resulted from state and federal responses to the recession and continued weak economic recovery. According to the Center on Budget and Policy Priorities, states are spending 28 percent less per student on higher education, nationwide, than they did in 2008 before the recession hit.[24] These cuts led to sharp increases in tuition, which affects college affordability and shifts the cost burden from state governments directly to the students. The College Board reports that the price of attending a four-year public college or university has grown significantly faster than the growth in median income within the last 20 years. Students face tuition costs that have risen faster than median family income, and are going into low-wage post-college jobs with nearly 30 grand in student loan debt - almost twice the amount it was in the 80's and 90's.[25] *Great Scott! We gotta go back to 1985!*

Another reason for rising costs is related to the increased payout for professors' sabbaticals, CEO's, and other administration on campus. The Delta Cost Project report found that in recent years, the average college or university has increased its institutional support (which includes general administrative services, executive management, legal and fiscal operations, and public relations) faster than it has increased its instructional and classroom expenditures.[26]

The rapid rise in enrollment also plays a part. Total undergraduate enrollment in degree-granting postsecondary institutions was 17.5 million students in the fall of 2013, an increase of 46 percent from 1990, when it was 12 million students. By 2024, total undergraduate enrollment is projected to increase to 19.6 million students.[27] This would logically lead to some increase in costs, as colleges expand and grow to offer enough classes for all the students, and pay for all the additional faculty and staff needed. Colleges also have to build facilities to house students, provide food and supplies for more people, and provide more health care (which is also increasing in cost) to faculty, staff and students. The cost of implementing new technologies, maintaining competitive programs and building new labs and student centers has also driven up the price of college.

While some state schools struggle with funds, others, like private colleges, raise their tuition every year just because they can. Colleges often use the rising tuition fees to provide the amenities that people are looking for on a campus. It is important to have safe living spaces and access to health care, food, and other resources on campus. We definitely need access to cutting edge technology. We need professors who create a valuable learning environment. But it seems that some colleges around America are just raising the cost of college to offer a lavish appeal.

I went to a private Texas university. At the time that I started looking at the college, it was within means, especially since I went to community college first. I also wanted the experience that often comes from a smaller school (less than 10,000), such as round table classroom discussions, and more one-on-one time with professors and advisors. Unfortunately, tuition was raised by six to eight percent every year. The whole time I was on campus, it was under construction. Classmates and I would joke that when something on campus was updated or new, that was where all our money was going. *"Hey look guys, my whole first semester's check probably paid for an 'I' on the new UNIVERSITY sign!"*

The improvements in my college's amenities were wonderful for the short period of time I was able to enjoy them. But as the costs went up, it made me wonder if the increase was largely to pay for those million dollar renovations that were not always associated with the learning experience. The campus today does not look anything like the one I explored at 17. In the course of five years, our student center was demolished and turned into a larger student union with more choices of food and a Starbucks. Old parking lots were filled with fresh new dorms, apartments and grand fountains. Old student lounges on campus were upgraded with better couches and recreational games. Every treadmill in the gym had a TV attached to it. The football stadium was torn down and rebuilt to expand the number of seats and add private boxes. New fitness facilities were built for the sports teams. The changes were beautiful and exciting, but were they all necessary?

A report released in February, 2009 by Public Agenda and the National Center for Public Policy and Higher Education highlights the public's loss of faith in colleges and universities.[28] Fifty three percent of Americans say that colleges could spend less and still maintain high-quality education. Fifty five percent say that higher education today is run like most businesses, with attention to the bottom line trumping the educational mission as a top priority.

Perpetuating inequality:

A divide keeps growing between those who earn a bachelor's degree by age 24 and those who don't. The percentage of students who earned a bachelor's degree from the lowest-income families—those making $34,160 a year or less— rose from only 6 percent in 1970 to 9 percent in 2013. College completion for students from the wealthiest families rose dramatically, though, climbing from 44 percent to 77 percent during the same time frame.[29]

For poor families, the ability to save for college is strenuous. For middle class families, living costs are rising so fast that saving is increasingly difficult. The costs of child care, higher education, health care, housing, and retirement rose by more than $10,000 in the twelve years between 2002 and 2012, while middle class incomes have largely remained stagnant.[30]

For the 20 percent at the top of the income spectrum, the cost of attending a public college has increased from six to nine percent of the total family income from 1971 to 2011. Yet, for the 20 percent at the bottom, the cost of public education has gone from 42 percent to 114 percent of the family income during the same period.[31] No wonder so many students in public universities drop out! The high attrition rate is not necessarily because of academic issues, but because people need to go back to the job market just to survive. People cannot survive on loans alone, knowing the risks involved with taking on more debt.

Why is the education system in America built to make society so unequal? Doesn't everyone deserve an equal shot in life by having access to affordable, high-quality education, especially when our world requires people to have some sort of education to prosper?

For-profit online colleges:

Many people do not have a traditional college experience. Perhaps because of financial burdens, the choice to start a family early, serve in the military, or just take some time to figure out what they want as a career. At some point, many decide they want to earn that degree they put on the backburner, so they enroll in online colleges. Most of these people are from low income families.

This type of online learning does, in fact, work for some people. There is also the argument that offering more online courses through traditional colleges can help cut some of the costs of school, and that we will see more of this online format in the future. Online courses can reduce costs, but may not be the most effective answer for the future of education in this country. A lot of the value of the college experience is based on the people you meet and the relationships you build with professors and other students. Learning how to work with peers and challenge each other is vital, and a precursor for the collaborative nature of many workplaces. Also, hands- on learning is invaluable in many fields.

In 2013, the news reported that online for-profit colleges were facing scrutiny on several fronts, but mainly the costs associated with for-profit and online schools, which enroll about 13 percent of all students in higher education.[32] It seems that many of these schools are leaving students with high debt and little return on investment based on their income after graduation. Many of these schools cost more than local community colleges and also do not provide the types of applied skills that students need for the real world.

These schools get a significant amount of funding from investors, but are also eligible to receive up to 90 percent of their funding from federal funds. That is taxpayer money! With for-profit schools largely funded by the government, the schools know they will receive money whether a student actually graduates or drops out. Their high push to promote is reflected in their expenditures. In 2009, the for-profit online colleges spent, on average, just 17.7 percent of their revenue on instruction, but 24.4 percent was spent on marketing and recruitment. In fact, in 2012, the University of Phoenix was the biggest spender on Google, spending approximately $170,000 *per day* on AdWords.[33] Disturbingly, pay to top executives at these types of schools averaged $7.3 million, which is well above that received by presidents at traditional schools, which averages in the $400,000 range.[34]

Even more astounding, 54 percent of the students who enrolled in for-profit colleges in 2008 and 2009 had dropped out by 2010. Many of these students, as well as those who did manage to finish, are burdened with debt.[35] In total, 96 percent of students at for-profit colleges have taken out loans, compared with about 50 percent at traditional four-year colleges, and just 13 percent at community colleges. Students enrolled in for-profit colleges only make up 13 percent of all students enrolled in a higher education institution of two or more years. However, 46 percent of all defaults on federal student loans came out of for-profit institutions.[36]

U.S. educational institutions are evaluated by, and receive accreditation from, private regional or national organizations, which entitle the schools to receive federal student aid. Federal officials are concerned that while institutions may be accredited on the national level, they may lack proper credentials from specialized organizations that accredit programs in particular fields. The U.S. Education Department has proposed eliminating federal funding for institutions with high proportions of graduates who default or whose debt levels are high relative to the graduates' incomes. The Consumer Financial Protection Bureau has worked with the Department of Education to determine whether some schools prod students into high-cost college loans, and simply extort them based on their desire to improve themselves.

Regulation and oversight of the for-profit college industry has increased in recent years, with enforcement of the "gainful employment" rule spurring the U.S. Department of Education to investigate job placement rates and dole out heavy fines to those misrepresenting career opportunities after college.[37] For-profit colleges have to show that they prepare students for "gainful employment in a recognized occupation," which is defined through a debt-to-income ratio. Colleges of all kinds should be held to a high standard of accountability.

In June of 2014, the Department of Education released a statement that made headlines, putting Corinthian Colleges, Inc., one of the largest for-profit colleges, under scrutiny.[38] Corinthian Colleges had received $1.4 billion annually from the federal government, mostly in the form of federal student loans and Pell Grants.[xiii] The colleges would be on an "increased level of financial oversight" because Corinthian had failed, several times, to hand over documents pertaining to its practices of using falsified job placement data to recruit prospective students and altering grades and graduation rates, and counting work at Taco Bell or becoming a waiter as justified, successful "in field" placement.[39] *Your parents (and bank account) might disagree.*

Enrollment seriously declined at Corinthian Colleges following the investigations by the Securities and Energy Commission, the Consumer Financial Protection Bureau, and several state attorneys generals. Understandably, the company's stock fell from $20 a share in 2010 to just under 30 cents a share in 2014. By 2015, the company had to cease all 28 of its operations.[40]

The University of Phoenix also reported losing nearly half of their students in the five-year period leading up to 2015. Strayer University

---

[xiii] A Pell Grant is money the government provides for students who need it to pay for college, which does not need to be paid back.

also reported a large loss of students during this time. The Arts Institutes, ITT Institute, DeVry University and Kaplan University all announced closures too.

The Corinthian downfall launched one of the largest student crises in the history of the Department of Education (ED). The ED had to discharge all student loan debts for Corinthian customers who were enrolled in a now-closed campus at any point in the 120 days prior to the closure. That "closed-school discharge" policy had only been used rarely in the past, and never at such magnitude. The ED approved loan discharges for some 8,800 former Corinthian students nationwide, totaling more than $130 million.[41]

The Obama administration announced in June 2016 it would overhaul the loan forgiveness process for students who believe they have been defrauded by their colleges, in light of the collapse of controversial for-profit Corinthian Colleges.[42] These students can apply to have their federal loans discharged if they can prove a school used illegal or deceptive tactics in violation of state law to persuade them to borrow money for college. But critics say the process, known as a "defense to repayment claim," is complicated and difficult to navigate. And the demise of Corinthian, with thousands of former students muddling their way through the claims process, has shown that the system needs improvement.[43] While students try to figure out what to do, they find that hidden in their enrollment contracts are mandatory arbitration clauses that bar students from filing class-action lawsuits or taking their grievances to court. It's a way for career schools to protect their financial interest. Perhaps if students had an easier time suing schools, they would be less likely to turn to the government for relief, saving taxpayers from picking up the tab for the misdeeds of private companies.

In a closed school discharge, if students get loans forgiven, they cannot keep their class credits. Those students can alternatively choose to transfer to a new school and keep their loans. Because transferring locks the student into repaying their full debt burden, it's a risky choice.[44] And for many, it may not even be an option, as many of these schools' credits do not transfer to other accredited colleges. It leaves them with no choice but to start all over again.

For-profit students can rarely transfer credits to traditional universities in the same way credits from community colleges transfer to a higher-level degree. Which begs the question, why would low-income students pay more for an education they could receive around the corner at a local community college? Why would they accumulate large amounts of debt to do it and forego the ability to transfer credits later? The high number of low-income students choosing to attend for-profit institutions signals a crisis in how our traditional community and public colleges are failing to serve low-income students.[45]

Detailed in an exploratory book, *After Admission: From College Access to College Success,* for-profit colleges often do a better job of attracting and enrolling students than community colleges. The book says that for-profits specifically train staff to reel students in, and then "pressure" them to quickly close the deal. Low-income students tend to have less familiarity with college options in general, and are more likely to have had negative experiences getting financial aid or information at traditional public institutions. Therefore, they tend to be easy targets. Once students express interest, the staff is trained in "intentional and explicit sales tactics" to shape what is termed an "admissions encounter" with students. The encounter is designed to get students to open up about individual hopes, fears, past experiences, and failures. Staff then capitalizes on this to convince them that their online college is the best solution, and may pressure the student to enroll on the spot, which includes providing all necessary financial aid paperwork.

It seems that some colleges have become another scam to avoid. The tactics used are much like those used on college graduates in past jobs I encountered. Does being young and hungry make us easy prey? Are some of these online schools more interested in harvesting federal money from taxpayers than they are in educating students? While it seems likely, the same question could also be asked about some traditional colleges as well.

Community colleges:

The purpose of community college is to provide a low-cost, flexible alternative to a four-year undergraduate degree. Students with jobs, children, and other responsibilities, who might not have time to devote to a bachelor's degree, can make a commitment to academics in a more flexible environment. One can receive vocational education at a community college to learn skills for a reasonable price. Some students, whose grades are not *all that* when applying to four-year institutions can improve credentials to better prepare for a four-year degree. Others can take time to earn basic credits at community college before making a final decision on next steps.

I attended community college when I was unsure of what I wanted to be and where my future was headed at just 17-years-old. By saving money on my basic core classes, I was able to better afford my top pick school and got accepted more easily (instead of wait-listed like I was the first time I applied right out of high school) after proving I could do well in college courses. It's also beneficial when schools offer student programs that allow juniors and seniors to attend community college during the last years of high school to earn college credits while still participating in high school activities. It helps young adults get slightly ahead of the game and reduces time spent earning a four year degree.

In President Obama's 2015 State of the Union address, he proposed two free years of community college for the American people. The plan would pay community colleges for academic programs that can transfer to four-year institutions and for vocational training programs for jobs in high demand. The proposal included a new American Technical Training Fund, which, according to the White House, was designed to "expand innovative, high-quality technical training programs." Because the new plan would eliminate tuition, students would be able to use Pell Grants for non-tuition expenses, including expensive text books, fees and living expenses. The proposal calls for increasing the amount of Pell Grants available to undergraduate students in all postsecondary institutions. This could potentially make college more affordable and decrease the amount of student debt.

While the thought of the nation's 1,100 community colleges becoming free for eligible students sounds great, it bears further examination. Will this be a way to alleviate the burden of the ever-increasing costs of college? Will curricula have to change significantly? Would this government-funded community college be the new 13th and 14th grade? Is providing free community college the government's way of admitting that K-12 is no longer "enough" to prepare us for university or qualify for a decent job? Will it do much to improve dropout rates at community colleges or encourage more transfer students to universities? These questions and more must be addressed so that a potentially free education better prepares students of tomorrow. Because unless these community classes meet the requirements to fill the jobs that are available, there will be a lot of people "cat walking" around with free degrees and lots of free time.

The White House said the proposal would cost $60 billion over the next ten years, which would be financed by hiking capital gains taxes on wealthy Americans and imposing a fee on large financial firms. Is this a viable option? Perhaps the recent attempts at the state level will lead the way for possibilities. Oregon and Tennessee are pioneers in this venture, and have recently made free community college the real deal, using money from lottery reserves. A blue northern state and red southern state coming together with common goals shows hope for the states as a whole.

The whole state of New York made headlines when it became the first state in the nation to make tuition free for students at both two- and four-year public colleges. Beginning in the fall of 2017, undergraduate students who attend a state school are eligible for the Excelsior Scholarship if their families earn no more than $100,000 a year. The income cap will lift to $110,000 in 2018 and will reach a cap of $125,000 in 2019. But like many "free college" proposals, this scholarship does not address the high cost of room and board.

This huge milestone has a caveat. After recipients graduate, they must work and live in New York for the same period of time they received financial assistance from the scholarship. If they don't live and work in the state, the scholarship becomes a loan. This makes it tricky for students to choose a grad school, or a job that is a better fit outside of the state. Regardless, New York is just trying to invest in their population today, to help grow their economy tomorrow.

College debt:

Determining how to lower college costs and avoid an impending student loan crisis has been a huge debate among the American people in these years following the Great Recession. Financial analysts vary in their opinions on what to do. Some proposed changes seem easy, while others will take re-evaluating the state of the entire system.

It would be helpful to expand education on education. The real meat of the problem is simply that students are taking on too much debt, without understanding the true costs of education. Providing more information about the links between college majors, graduation rates, education debt, and employment outcomes is important. Schools themselves should be educating students on how to handle student loans. Student debt becomes a real burden when students don't graduate or if graduates can't get jobs that provide a salary that allows them to pay back the loans. We need to stop making it so easy for students to accrue endless amounts of debt. Students should be educated on the real costs of college, fair interest rates, and what their monthly loan repayment amounts will look like. The real world financial impact needs to be understood by students and their families *before* taking out loans.

Students should be made aware of other options to pay for college via grants or scholarships, which do not need to be repaid. Websites like FastWeb.com (FinAid's sister site) and CollegeScholarships.org help parents and students find other alternatives to pay for college instead of traditional loans. This may be a little extra work, but grants and scholarships can be a great way to make college more affordable. A few thousand dollars here and there can help with the cost of books and labs. Just a quick search on the web will find you scholarship opportunities for weird things like best duck call, cutest prom couple, and prompts to write essays on what it is like to be very tall or live at a nudist colony.

It can be argued that four years of college is too long for some majors. Some degrees could easily be compressed into three years, cutting off a year's worth of costs. But a large problem is that most people do not even graduate within four years. Only 36.5 percent of students at public, four-year universities have obtained a degree after five years—close to the lowest level in three decades. That number does go up at private universities, where 57 percent graduate within five years according to an analysis by ACT, which has kept a comprehensive database of completion rates since 1983.[46] Perhaps we should focus on increasing rates of timely graduation, instead of just looking at ways to cut classes from the curriculum.

Completing college level courses while still in high school could shave off semesters of expensive education at a fraction of the cost. High school students should seek out AP (advanced placement) level courses to earn college credits that easily transfer to universities. Also, internships or part-time jobs that entail learning skills useful for future jobs and careers should translate to college credits.

Arguments are made that the billions of dollars the government spends on student loans would be better spent going directly to the schools, rather than putting students in debt to cover the costs. A plan for government oversight could allow for limits on tuition, and ensure funds are going toward bettering education, not frivolous expenditures. By subsidizing public higher education, it could incentivize private ones to reduce their costs in order to compete with the more affordable options.

While these ideas could help make college more affordable for future students, it does nothing to help struggling borrowers who have already graduated, or those who have dropped out of school with high levels of student loan debt. Many people argue that Congress should repeal the exception to bankruptcy discharges for federal and private student loans. If the federal government and private lenders choose to make student loans, they should also accept the risks inherent in lending.

Needless to say, college grads are desperate to have our student loans disappear, which explains the rise in scams that prey on naive and needy, in-debt graduates. These scams have been found readily advertising on Google Ads or Facebook, and claim that for a small fee they can get students out of debt. They promise students they can cut student loan payments by 50 percent or more. They take advantage of students' lack of knowledge about repayment options and the lack of intervention by student loan services. The Consumer Financial Protection Bureau's student loan ombudsman, Seth Frotman, said student loan debt scammers are strikingly similar to the mortgage relief scammers of the recession.

The Federal Reserve Bank of New York estimates that out of the nearly 40 million borrowers, about seven million have defaulted on these student debts.[47] That means millions have trashed credit as a result of student loans and can have 25 percent in penalties added onto their total student loan debts.[48] To add insult to injury, when employers run credit checks on applicants before hiring or promoting them, if bad credit is found, the employer can make a decision not to move forward with the job offer, and that makes it difficult for many to get a higher paying job to actually repay student debts.

Many people do not know their options when it comes to repaying student loans, and loan companies have no incentive to educate people about these programs. One prudent way to help is to link repayment to income: The more you earn, the faster you pay back the loan. If college doesn't pay off, you pay less. One of the best ways to lower student loan payments is by applying for an income-driven repayment plan. In June 2014 the Obama administration announced a cap on Federal student loan borrower's payments at 10 percent of income. This cap alleviates some debt, and helps some to pursue meaningful careers "while avoiding consequences of defaulting on a Federal student loan, such as a damaged credit rating, a tax refund offset, or garnished wages."[49]

Access to higher education is tremendous, but the burdens placed on students and the constant rise of tuition is reckless. Regardless of how and why it's happening, something must be changed. College is supposed to open up possibilities, not be the weight in the way of prosperity.

It takes hard work to get into a good college: above average grades in high school, high marks on the SAT or ACT, involvement in extracurricular activities, and a plan to pay tuition. If students are working this hard, we should be asking questions like, which colleges will provide a good return on our investment to the majority of the population of students they serve? Which schools will teach the skills needed to flourish in the fields? What colleges have high graduation and job placement rates and low student debt loads? It is a common misconception that a higher tuition means a higher quality educational experience. The fact that many college graduates struggle to pay their loans is one more reason for us to worry about the cost of tuition, not to doubt the value of getting a higher education.

College rankings:

In August 2013 President Obama proposed a new college ratings system called the "College Scorecard." The government website, which launched in 2015, identifies and ranks schools that offer the best value in an effort to help students and families make more informed decisions about which college to attend. Students can compare schools on cost, graduation rates, loan default rates, and even how much students earn after graduation.

It's easier now to see that not all colleges are created equal. The college ratings system is a way like never before for consumers to read reviews, compare facts, and weed out the obviously less desirable colleges. Although the Scorecard offers up important data points to know and understand, these do not take into account all aspects of a quality education. It's great that the government is trying to hold all types of schools accountable for the education they provide, but it is difficult to have an evaluation system that fits all, especially when colleges vary in terms of what they have to offer. Every school has its own strengths, weaknesses and specialties that may not be thoroughly captured in such a rating system.

Over time, open access to consumer insights and data will have to become standard so that students can be better informed about the best education pathway. It may also incentivize colleges to collaborate with employers to develop programs that help shape students into desirable employees, which could help their rankings. It has been brought up by the Association of Public and Land-grant Universities that a lot of key data on the Scorecard is incomplete and misleading (such as graduation rates and earnings) due to a congressional ban on student-level data. If Congress passed a pending bill called the College Transparency Act, it would enable the College Scorecard website to post much more detailed and accurate data, and help the future of American college students.

Are we learning?

With the rising costs of education comes hype about the actual value of a college education, begging the question: what are we getting out of college? In 2013, a study found the average literacy level of American college graduates is below the average literacy level of that same cohort in other nations.[50] Around the same time, a book titled *Academically Adrift: Limited Learning on College Campuses* was published, questioning whether students are really learning in college.[51] The book and its corresponding report document research findings that followed 2,300 undergraduates through four years of college (at 24 unidentified but academically representative institutions), to measure progress in their critical thinking and analytic reasoning skills.

The book's authors drew many conclusions from their research, perhaps the most shocking of which is that 36 percent of students demonstrated no significant gains in critical thinking, complex reasoning, and written communication over four years of college. This means that 64 percent of students did show improvement, but that is a 'D' grade in most classrooms. The measurement tool was the "Collegiate Learning Assessment," which the students took during their freshman, sophomore and senior years. The CLA consists of open-ended questions, is administered to students online.

But the CLA is just another standardized test. While it measures for important skills, the CLA may not be constructed to adequately reflect how much specialized knowledge has actually been learned because it focuses on general skills rather than domain knowledge and specialization. Educators still have much to learn about what to teach and how students best learn.

With the large number of young adults unable to find good jobs, and the news stories of college students not actually significantly learning, there have been charges by the public that the American education system is not upholding its prestigious history or reputation for valuable academic learning. When outstanding student loan debt crossed the $1 trillion threshold, it had a huge effect on the national dialogue, making us question if college is worth all the time and money. It made many question whether college is a joke.

But education is not the joke. The joke is the inefficiency and lack of action. If students are only opting for the easy classes on Ratemyprofessor.com and not studying or getting involved in classes, and if faculty members are not demanding enough of students, and administrators are not paying attention to student learning outcomes, and if the federal government isn't awarding grant money to figure out why students aren't learning, and if the money spent by administrators is not put toward learning programs, then no one is doing their job correctly and no one will get what they want! *Whew... that is a lot of needed accountability!*

College is an exciting and challenging experience for students, but for some, it is simply too much to handle. Few high school students are aware of what college life is like, and what it actually takes to get through. Procrastination and poor time-management skills can lead to more time spent partying than studying, a main cause of failing tests. While students can initially set out study goals, it's easy to fall into the party scene, as Greek life, sports, and social gatherings dominate many campuses. Any student who has a typical college experience can attest to the great emphasis on partying in college: dorm parties, college night at the local bars, beer pong tournaments, themed parties and more. While fun and part of the "experience", these are ultimately distractions and can take away from the true reason kids should be in college. Are we paying just to party? We can't all afford to be the next Van Wilder, taking years and years to graduate, and taking the line from said movie "Don't be a fool, stay in school!" to a ridiculous level.

Lists of the "Top Party Schools" come out every year. While jumping off roofs into pools, and building a record breaking beer tower make epic stories, basing one's choice of college on the party scene rather than the academics is a real issue amongst students that are young and impressionable. This population can easily fall victim to the party scene, causing many to fall behind in studies, fail courses, flunk out entirely, or worse, suffer health-related problems or injuries. College students continue to drink heavily, even after repeated bad experiences, because of the social opportunities it provides. Those who are not into the party scene are often left out or do not feel like part of the community. Students want to have fun and feel a part of something in the present, but this often negatively impacts futures and goals.

Is college worth it?

As social issues continue to change in this day and age, the media is flooded with articles asking this simple question: *Is college worth it?* I would argue college is worth the return if you manage to graduate *and* if you do so without taking on unmanageable debt. I also feel that college is worth the time, if you not only learn and get put on a path to finding a good job, but also take advantage of the experiences and opportunities a college campuses offer up.

College is what you make of it. It's helpful to know your goals and know where you are going and how you will get there. College is a way to prove to yourself and future hiring managers that you can commit to something. College is a way to be a step ahead of the competition, if you use it to your advantage. But much of what you learn in college is not just set by the curriculum, syllabus and tests you take. College is a life experience that is hard to compare to anything else. Working with activists on campus, finding groups and friends with similar interests, and going to symposiums and lectures from experts or famous people are wonderful opportunities. Having access to new technology, labs, one-on-ones with professors, professionals in the field, or mentors is invaluable.

College is not a walk in the park for many people. Between balancing part-time jobs, going to 12 to 18 hours of classes a week, all the hours spent at the library working on projects and papers and studying for tests, plus extracurricular activities, and social events, it is not uncommon to feel overwhelmed. We must learn to balance the fun with hard work. Part of learning in college is realizing that not all lessons are taught in the classroom. College is a place where you can discover your values, and what interests you, so you will become a well-rounded individual. One can argue that college is not only about classes, but about maturing, meeting different kinds of people, making connections, and making mistakes. But it sure can be an expensive lesson in finding yourself.

Whatever we choose to do, we should hold ourselves accountable for our decisions. It has become apparent that we cannot rely solely on schools or policymakers to help us figure out the right path. When faced with the future, young adults should ask questions like: *Why am I going to college? If college isn't in the cards, what play is next? Where am I going and how will I get there? What can I do to look out for myself to make sure that I do not become lost in the system? What are some jobs I would like to do, and what are the steps I need to take to get there? What will make me stand out as a tiger in this world full of house cats?*

In life, you always have to choose what is most important to you. And once you decide what is important, you always find the time in your life for it. And if you don't, then it probably isn't that important to you. For instance, you may say you want to be a graphic designer, but you don't make any time to design for fun, take classes, read books or watch videos, or seek out freelance work. So, maybe you have misguided yourself a bit.

To succeed in today's job market you either need to find something you are passionate about and pursue it relentlessly, or you need to do your research on what kind of jobs are actually out there, and prepare for them. It's okay to major in a subject that is not one of the STEM subjects. It may be a little harder to find a job, but it is not impossible. In the end, you have to make the best decision for yourself. Go with your instincts. Just find something you feel strongly about and let those gut feels guide you. If you plan to base your career on what you study, think about the fact that it will affect how you spend much of your waking time for the rest of your life. If a certain standard of living is important to you, find out what you have to do to make that a reality before you waste years studying something that will not get you closer to living the life you want to live.

What I wish I had known when I was in school is that you can't trust the curriculum outlines 100 percent. You have to step up and do your own research on what jobs are out there, figure out exactly what skills you need, and seek out relevant and available programs and classes. Read job postings to see the skills needed to get the types of jobs you want, then study and perfect those skills. Make a "wish list" resume that you wish was yours. Figure out ways to make that resume go from fiction to nonfiction. We need portfolios, ideas and innovations, and technical skills in order to stand out. Get involved, meet people who do similar work, join organizations, and practice at subjects and affairs that make you happy.

Additionally, many young adults would benefit by taking some time between high school and college to work and find out pros and cons about certain jobs. Sometimes a little real-world experience is the push young adults need to take going to college more seriously instead of wasting valuable time and money on being "unsure." Working jobs you are not a fan of can be a motivator to help figure out what your next step should be. Travel, interning, volunteering, and doing a bit of self-studying are all ways you can take a deeper look inside to find out where you potentially belong. It also can be an opportunity to fine tune some of those soft and hard skills. In many ways, having relative experience to put on a resume is more helpful than just college classes.

It is unrealistic to say that everyone can go to college or that college is right for everyone. When graduation approaches, young people should not be automatically set up for a life of debt. Guidance from counselors on when it is best to choose public versus private college, or a different type of skills learning in general, like trade schools or how to earn certifications. For many people, there is a stigma against not having a college degree or not working a traditional job. But with so many high-paying skilled trades jobs that need filling, we need to increase interests in these careers. Aircraft mechanics, air traffic controllers, service managers, plumbers, and electricians are all high-paying skilled trades that are in high demand.

Regardless of major, the unemployment rate for college graduates is still considerably lower than that of non-college graduates. Compare these statistics: unemployment (by government standards) averages 8.9 percent for college graduates, 22.9 percent for high school graduates, and a staggering 31.5 percent for high school dropouts. Even in a saturated, unstable job market, a college degree helps. Higher education can be a good investment, you just have to be smart with your decisions about where to go, what to study, and how much to pay.

Chapter 9

Family Roomies

In the year's following the recession, a record number of young Americans live with family members, with realizations of just how tough it can be to make it on your own. In other countries, multiple generations living under one roof is the norm. Families help each other out with multiple incomes to be able to have the quality of life they want. By contrast, in America, there is still a stigma about rooming with your parents in your twenties; a social perception that living at home means you are lazy or somehow deficient. But there is a difference between a twentysomething who is getting help from her parents while actually trying to become financially independent, versus someone who just sits at home and eats Cheetos all day long. We are not all a bunch of LUFs (lazy unemployed felines). Many people just do not have another option, as job opportunities can be scarce immediately after graduation. And the reminders of student loan debt come knocking just six months after graduation. It is often a more viable option to live with your family than to live with strangers you aren't sure you can trust. Even so, moving back in with your parents due to the economy can hinder feelings of true independence because of the lack of personal space or financial security.

A Pew Research study called "Young, Underemployed and Optimistic," found that younger Millennials (ages 18-24) are much more likely to be living with parents; more than half of the people in that age group have either returned to the nest, or never left. Among the general population, Pew Research says that 41 percent of people think young adults have it tougher than anyone in the current job market, and a growing number of parents say they believe children should aim for economic independence by age 25, rather than a younger age.[52] But even age 25 is beginning to seem young, as more people are living at home into our late twenties and early thirties.

Another reason so many young people end up living at home is that it is hard to find a rental property that is both affordable and livable. Rental prices keep rising because the demand for rentals keeps growing, and that's partly because fewer people can afford to buy homes now than we could before the recession. The banks increased regulations and restrictions after the housing bubble burst due to their risky lending practices. The low supply of rentals has created a situation in which people who definitely can't afford to buy are also priced out of renting. The tightening rental market has the most significant impact on low-income renters. Many high- and middle-income renters occupy units that are affordable to lower income groups, reducing the supply of decent, affordable, available apartments for the lowest income renters. In my apartment searches, I discovered how difficult it is to find an affordable place to live that was not the size of a closet, falling apart, or infested with bugs. According to 2014 data from the National Low Income Housing Coalition, for every 100 extremely low income renter households, there were just 31 affordable and available units.

Without anywhere to go after graduating, I moved back in with my parents. My first chance to step into adulthood, and I reverted back to 18-years-old. In fact, most of my close friends did. Other friends moved in with a significant other or roommates because it was just too hard to find an affordable place to live alone. My goal was to be able to squirrel away as much money as possible in a savings account so I could bust out one day.

But in the early years, this savings account didn't exist because I was not making much money. And every penny I made went to paying bills and student loans. It is now a recurring theme that many college graduates are spending our first ten years out of college paying off student loan debt, rather than saving or investing. According to Debt.org, the average college senior graduates with $25,000 to $30,000 in student loan debt with a ten year loan. When I finally got to a point where I was able to start saving, it felt as though my money was more like video game points in the game of life. I rarely saw real cash or a check. Money just went directly from my employers to my bank account, then bills were automatically deducted from there, while small amounts were automatically placed in a savings account. It was all about building enough "points" to survive. But as time went on and layoffs happened and jobs ended, I was stuck using up most of my savings just to get by. Every time I felt I had enough money to move out, something dramatic would happen.

I come from a "middle class family," which I put it in quotations because that is what the government has coined us, and not how we view ourselves.[xiv] My first crib was a dresser drawer. Don't worry; I got a real bed eventually! We have confusion about perception versus reality when it comes to Americans and our social classes. Many do not even know or understand social grouping, as everyone lives a different perceived reality. Just because two different families make the same income does not mean that both families have the same quality of life. Every family or individual has different expenses, obligations, blessings, and burdens.

My dad left his home at 18-years-old to join the Navy because he didn't have another option growing up in farmland Maine. His mother had passed when he was 13, and he was left with no safety net. After the Navy, he got a job at Hughes Aircraft Company, was given financial aid through his job, and started college in southern California at the age of 26 where he earned an electrical engineering degree.

My mother also did not have a financial safety net as she grew up with four other siblings. She studied some at a community college and lived out of her car for a short period while trying to make it in her twenties. *Boy,*

[xiv] According to Investopedia, the income distributions fall as follows for a family of four: Upper class $250,000+, Upper- middle class $150,000+, Middle class $100,000+, Lower-middle class $35,500-$60,000, Lower class $23,050-$32,500, and Poverty is $23,050 or less.

am I glad it never came to that for me. My dad came along, and with two incomes, they were able to do better. My dad worked his way from the bottom up, made smart decisions, investments, and sacrifices so he could raise our family of four in a comfortable environment. My mom ultimately became a stay-at-home mom so she could raise my younger sister and me. She volunteered at our schools in the PTA and helped with fundraisers.

My parents enrolled us in dance, gym, and art classes, and took us to the library every week where I would pile up as many books as possible to take home. They spent time doing crafts and homework with us, and my father showed great patience when I came home crying over my math homework. They took us to museums, encouraged learning different cultures, and divulged many life lessons. They also took us to church, where we were part of the choir and youth groups. They encouraged us to be creative and to find our true selves.

Living at home for me was not a bad prospect, because I got along with my parents most of the time. My sister, Hayley, and I held a more delicate dynamic, often having outbursts about stupid stuff as many sisters do. But for some people, living at home as a young adult is unbearable. And others do not even have that as an option. Not everyone has a cozy nest to jump back into when times get tough. I was privileged to be raised by two amazing people who understood what I was going through. I was also lucky that at my parents' house, the whole upstairs was pretty much mine and my younger sister's territory.

The best parts about living at home, for me, were the occasional home-cooked meal, a fully stocked fridge, and free Wi-Fi and cable. The house was always as warm or as cool as I would want it to be. There was always someone around to try new recipes out on, remind me that I needed to work out, or drive me to the airport. If I forgot to wash my dishes or do my laundry, it might even be done by the time I got home, with no passive aggressive sticky note to go along with the favor. In retrospect, my parents were the most mature and easy-to-live-with roommates I have ever had. But it was still difficult to feel like a responsible and independent person when I felt like a high school aged kid living at home in a full house, all four of us back under one roof.

I'm sure many twentysomethings can relate to some of the incidents me, my sister, and even some of my friends went through while living back at home.

Spatial issues:

My parents did not leave the house much. My dad works from home and my mom has been a homemaker since I was born. My mother is one of those people who is always in the same place at the same time as you. Need to fill the water bottle? Guess who is right behind you breathing on your neck? Making a sandwich? Gee... what a coincidence that she wants one at the same time! Want to wash your face late at night? Guess who is standing outside of your bathroom watching you like a cat creeping in the darkness stalking its prey.

Household projects or chores:

When living at home, your parents may or may not make you pay rent. My parents did not expect me to pay rent after I moved back in after college. But they did expect me and my sister to involve ourselves in household projects. Stuff constantly needed to be updated or cleaned. We helped refinish furniture, build a fence and paint several walls. I felt like Tom Sawyer! These were tasks I would not necessarily have made myself do. My parents joked that the reason they'd even had kids was to have their own personal helpers.

I will say, it's always nice to have access to a free washer and dryer. You might even be lucky enough to have a parent who wants to do your laundry for you—unless you wake up late for work and discover your mom decided to wash your uniform at the exact time you need to be wearing it . . .

I do not mind doing my laundry. In fact, I always say that *a load of laundry a day keeps the clutter away!* Sometimes, when I have a lot going on in my life, I can change outfits several times in one day: from work clothes, to active wear, to casual clothes, to date night, to pajamas. Needless to say, that adds up to a lot of laundry. But there were times when I was living at home when Mom decided to be "nice" and crept into my room to get some towels or other clothes to add to the wash. Towels were okay, but what didn't make me happy is when she would wash garments that maybe didn't need to be washed… like my "skimpy" underwear… which she then made fun of me for! *Boundaries people!* But at least my laundry was not left wet on top of the dryer, which is common at an apartment or dorm when someone wants to use the washer your clothes are still in at the end of the wash cycle. *Aargh.*

Family meetings:

No matter how mature you get, parents always want to have serious chats about your future. This is especially the case when they are able to see the struggles you are going through first-hand. My parents liked to host family meetings in our living room, which was different from the family room. Only visits with special guests, Christmas, and family meetings took place in the living room. My parents were always interested in what my bills added up to and what I was spending money on. They constantly wanted to know about my job status, trying to determine whether I was making the most of my time. They wanted to know how I spent my free time and who I was dating. My dad complained, "We hardly see you!"—even though I lived with them! They made it a point to remind me that they missed me when I would leave for a few hours. They seemed to have forgotten what it was like to be in their twenties and have a need to get out of the house, and be away from parental influences. But I learned that if someone cares this much about what is going on with me, it must be a good thing. I'm lucky to have such caring parents. I realize some people don't.

Belongings:

Living with a sibling is different than living with a friend, because with a sibling you are not afraid to just put it out there and say it like it is. My sister and I are each other's best friends and worst enemies. We mostly got along growing up, and the older we get, the three years, three months, and three days between us seems smaller and smaller. But as young women we would often get into situations that were tense. Especially since my sister could be considered a klepto! Everything within her reach in that house she considered fair game. Even when we were little, she would take my clothes, shoes and make-up and not return them. I often found myself acting like a scavenger in her room, trying to find shirts or necklaces of mine that was missing. I usually did not have to look too hard, as my stuff was just strewn across her floor.

When taking a shower in the morning I'd find my shampoo or face wash missing so I would have to scurry wearing only a towel through the upstairs to grab it out of her shower. Nothing is more infuriating than being wet, cold, and naked, running around your parents' house trying to find your own hygiene products at an ungodly early hour of the morning. I never got used to this happening over and over again. It gets worse when your sibling or parent accidentally sees you naked...

At one point or another, when Mom is cleaning your room— you know, just for shits and giggles—she may come across some unsavory objects that you like to keep private. My sister was horrible at hiding paraphernalia she did not want to be found. Goods always got discovered—mostly because everyone was always in her room trying to find our own damn possessions! Let's just say we always knew when she had experimented with drugs or just where the Cheez-It box disappeared to.

One of my friends, who was also living with her parents, told me how she'd accidentally left her vibrator and a *Harry Potter* book out on her bed one day while attending community college classes. She was freaking out about her parents finding the half-read book. Not the vibrator, you ask? Oh, that was the least of her worries. Her parents were against the topics of witchcraft, wizardry and Halloween. She feared their reaction to the *Harry Potter* book and how much trouble she would be in. Not so many worries about vibrator, as they probably wouldn't even have known what it was, she said.

Pretty sure the two objects were not related. But if you're into that... I wish you a magical time.

Food:

Don't even get me started on all the times my yogurt or pizza went missing out of the refrigerator. In fact, nothing in the fridge was safe, and anything nonperishable would have to be hidden in my room so that no one else would eat it. I was not only trying to squirrel away money, but also food! When you have roommates, you can write your name on your food and then get pissed off at them for eating it, because it was clearly marked. At your parents' house, everything is fair game. I had to get used to the fact that just because I bought myself some organic fruit did not mean I would get to eat it. It's hard to make an argument when you are eating their free food all the time! It's kind of embarrassing how many times I had to rant and rave over my yogurt being eaten because I didn't like the kind my mom bought. It also made it hard to plan meals or budget when it was a mystery as to what would actually be left in the fridge by day's end.

Visitors and parties:

When I lived with my parents there were times during the night when everyone had to be quiet. My parents' bedtime was 10:00 every night and, like clockwork, the house would be dark by then. Having people over past that hour on weekends was hard, given that I am a naturally loud person and my mother is a naturally light sleeper. My mother could wake at the tiniest sliver of light coming in through the cracks of her door, or at the sound of the TV on volume level three! I learned to either be quiet or risk seeing my braless mother come downstairs in front of my friends. Worse, my mother's revenge for waking her up was to vacuum right outside my bedroom at 8:00 on a Saturday morning!

My parents usually went out of town every summer to travel the U.S., visiting friends and family along the way. They would be gone for weeks at a time, leaving Hayley and I with the tabbies. At first, even though we were in our early twenties, they would have a family friend stay at the house with us. Having a 60-year-old man who is not your dad live with you can be quite awkward. You can't just go downstairs in your robe. You can't just have people over. And the quiet hours still apply! We were desperate to get our parents to leave us alone in the house. Sometimes, my sister and I were able to get our "sitter" to leave for the weekend so we could have people over.

But for a couple of summers, our parents left us by ourselves. I like my quiet time, and would usually go out to see my friends instead of having them at the house. My sister would constantly have people over. Every time I went downstairs I would find beers bottles strewn across counters, cigarette butts in the backyard, and random articles of clothing that had been left behind... and sometimes an actual person passed out on one of our couches. *Maybe that is why we had a chaperone . . .* At times, I would get annoyed with all the people coming and going, feeling like I had no privacy. Other times, I was thankful for the free beer and food that was brought into the house by my sister's friends. The get-togethers were always fun, as music echoed through the house and fun games were played. I met a lot of interesting people during those summers, as my sister's friends were from different walks of life than my usual friends.

Dating:

The hardest part about living at home for me was dating. After my college boyfriend and I broke up, I had to worry about starting from scratch; revealing embarrassing information about myself that wasn't an issue before. To tell or not to tell the new guy I was dating that my roommates were the people who had conceived me—that was the question. Would they wonder why I always drove to meet them on their side of town? When was it okay to tell, and how would I even break the news? Should I go on pretending that I could never bring anyone back to my place because I had crazy roomies? Would he think I was trying to hide the fact that I was a hoarder? And just how long would I have to keep lugging around a mini-bathroom in my purse so I would always be prepared for a long night?

Luckily, when I explained the situation most of the good guys understood, or would reveal that they also had lived at home.

Improvised sleepovers were a struggle. To pull it off, I tried to perfect the art of sneakiness and the quietness of a cat's pitter patter. But neither was my forte. Now, I didn't bring many guys back to my parents' mostly because, well, I didn't have that many dates. But there were a couple of times I had someone sleep over and then tried to sneak him out at 5:30 a.m. It was quite a challenge. My early-bird mother always knew. It became too embarrassing and it was too much of a hassle to make it worthwhile.

I had a some friends who lived at home with their parents after college, and also had their boyfriend or girlfriend live there too. I don't know how they handled seeing their parents every day while trying to make a full-time adult relationship work under their parents' roof. I can't help but wonder how the "adult" time worked. Did their parents ever recognize the sounds, or did they attribute it to feral cats?

Yes, living with parents as a grown adult can definitely be (insert jazz hands) *awkward*.

Chapter 10

94 To 100 Degrees Or Bust!

Anyone who has ever accepted a job knows you have a chance of being subjected to a drug test before you get to complete the acceptance papers. Opinions and debates about this issue are abundant. On one hand, people complain this is an invasion of privacy and that employers have no right to know what people do on their own time, as long as it is, in fact, their own time and not the company's time. On the other hand, it is easy to understand that employers want dedicated workers. The employers have the perception that an employee who does drugs will not meet their work quality and expectations, so this is one way to partially screen for whether this person would what they consider a "good employee." If the company is offering health insurance, it could often be the insurance companies that request this information. Drug testing is expensive for companies. It could cost them anywhere from $25 to $100 to get a person screened. It's a loss if the person fails. It's also a hassle to the potential employee. No one wants to be treated like a criminal and forced to pee into a cup in a cold room.

Drug testing is mostly a threat to those who smoke marijuana. THC—the chemical in marijuana that gets you high—sticks to fat cells, and therefore stays in your system longer than any other drug. A person could do cocaine, ecstasy, or even heroin, and most likely their system would be clean within a few days. A marijuana smoker could take weeks to months to get the drug out of their system. This isn't necessarily fair to the people who have an occasional toke just like they would have an occasional drink.

But cannabis still has a bit of a negative reputation to some. Some thinkers believe in the "Big Bong Theory," saying, "Young people are unemployed because they are too high to get hired!" *The unemployment rate is so high it has the munchies!*

It's true that cannabis is the most widely used drug in the world, with 68 percent of Millennials surveyed by Pew Research stating it should be legal.[53] In 2012, two states made history by legalizing recreational use of marijuana: Washington and Colorado. Other states started to follow suit and by 2016, Oregon, D.C., Alaska, California, Maine, Massachusetts, and Nevada had all legalized marijuana for personal use; another 28 states had legalized medical use.[54]

Arguably—and ironically—legalizing marijuana has been a way to create jobs, educational programs and to build better schools. For example, in Colorado, tax revenue collected from the sale of recreational marijuana is deposited in two different funds: the Building Excellent Schools Today

(BEST) Fund and the Marijuana Tax Cash Fund (MCTF). The first 40 million in tax revenue goes directly to the BEST fund every year. The MCTF is put toward health care, health education, substance abuse prevention and treatment programs, and law enforcement.[55]

But even though the laws have decriminalized cannabis use in those states and you may go buy it over the counter for recreational use, you can still be fired or not hired if weed shows up on your drug test. In states where marijuana is legal for medical use, an employer can still refuse to hire you even if you have a doctor's prescription.

The number of websites that discuss how to clear the body of THC within a limited time are vast. People make money off of desperate marijuana users. There are a number of companies that manufacture and market synthetic urine or detox drinks that guarantee passing a drug test. I do know a few people who have passed company and government issued drug tests by using the right detox drinks.

I don't think smoking marijuana makes one a bad person or a lazy employee. I think if it is used under the same guidelines and restrictions applied to alcohol, it can help people relax or even evoke creativity. All the pot users I know do not feel the need to be high at all times, and are smart and mature enough not to do it on work time or even advertise, while in a professional setting, that they use it. The argument that smoking weed makes people lazy may be valid. I mean, sure, they might even be so high and lazy that they pour the milk directly in the cereal box because all the bowls are dirty. But if not done on the job, does it affect productivity?

Attitudes toward pot have become more accepting with every generation. It has become less taboo, and is even endorsed by successful people. It is not the scary "wacky tabacky" other generations knew it as, but more like a natural substance from the earth that has many uses, such as making paper, oil, fuel, wax, clothes, food, medicine and, of course, helping people relax.

Like many, I have occasionally enjoyed marijuana as a way to relax and to calm the stress brought on by life. There were a few times, especially during the worst stretches of unemployment, when I decided to partake with my friends in smoking a bowl. Like a feline enjoying catnip, it was all in good fun and did no harm to anyone. We usually sat around watching movies or talking about life, love and other mysteries.

After I had quit a scammy job, I desperately and diligently looked for work. I was so broke I was literally counting nickels and dimes I had collected in a junk drawer. Suddenly, I found myself cornered in a situation in which I had to make a tricky choice that would decide my fate.

A week after a smoke with friends,[xv] I was invited for a game changing interview. It paid more than I had ever made with opportunities for commissions, and included the freedom to plan my own day. At the end of my rounds of interviews, I was offered the job, on the condition that I pass a background check and take a drug test. My heart sank. Suddenly, I felt like a terrible person; like I should have known better than to smoke weed while searching for work. But I was in grave need of a job.

[xv] This was before any state recreational legalizations of the plant.

That's when I considered my options. I had to decide between being honest and losing out on a career opportunity, or faking a drug test so I could take an opportunity for which I had been waiting a long time. I could turn down the job because of impending failure, but to me that just was not an option at all, so I tossed that thought aside. I could drink a detox drink, but I had heard mixed reviews about the outcomes. I could get a clean urine sample from a friend, but that seemed embarrassing to ask for, as well as downright gross. My last option was to buy synthetic urine, which a few people I knew had used to pass drug tests. First stop after the interview was the nearest smoke shop to get the pee kit. It cost around $40 and came with everything I needed: the faux urine, an easy-to-hide bottle with a pour nozzle with a temperature strip on it, a mini heating pad, and a rubber band. All I had to do was heat the liquid solution in the microwave for a few seconds, and it would stay at the perfect urine temperature of 94 to 100 degrees. It couldn't be too hot or too cold, because then it would be an automatic failure.

I left the house wearing a sports bra and baggy tee shirt and had all my supplies hot and ready in hand. It was a ridiculously hot summer day in Texas, one where as soon as you stepped outside you could get a farmer's tan. I nervously made my way to the nearest drug testing facility, sweating from an unidentifiable combination of nerves and heat. After I pulled in the parking lot, I carefully placed the bottle under my armpit in my sports bra and skittishly walked into the lab. As I explained what I was there for, the lady at the front desk told me that I was at the wrong location and that the location that did pre-employment drug testing was 30 minutes away. *Suffering Succotash!* I didn't want the fake urine to get below 94 degrees, so I went out to my car and wrapped the bottle in the heating pad just in case.

Turns out I didn't have to worry about that. My monkey-flunking air conditioning broke on the way to the second location! My mind rushed with grave thoughts. I became so sweaty and red that I looked like I had just eaten a level five hot wing! Not only that, but my fake pee was actually overheating! The monitor read 104 degrees! I thought, *That's not a normal human temperature—I'm surely doomed!*

I just kept thinking about how much I needed this job and how now I also needed to fix my car. It wasn't like my fake pee was hurting anyone, I told myself. I knew I was a dedicated hard worker, and I wasn't going to be thrown under the unemployment bus because of a few good times with my friends. I rushed into the nearest popular fast food joint and asked for an ice water. I was drenched in sweat and my heart was beating out of my chest. After chugging down some of the water, I got back to my car and dipped the bottle of synthetic urine into the ice-cold water for a few seconds. The temperature dropped down to a perfect 100 degrees. I was ready to do this!

I walked into the correct facility and I was greeted by refreshingly cold air-conditioning and a grumpy lady who treated me like a delinquent, even though this was only a pre-employment screening. *Did she know?!* She led me back to the bathroom, told me to empty my pockets and leave my purse outside the room. She said I only had three minutes to complete the task.

The sink in the bathroom did not even work, because (I assume) of the risk of people diluting their urine. As soon as I made it in the restroom, I checked the temperature again. *Still perfect!* As I peed in the toilet, I poured the solution into the test cup, right up to the limit.

After I finished my business, the first item of business the grumpy tech did was test the temperature of the cup. I had heard that if I passed this part I was almost guaranteed to pass. Facilities use synthetic urine for testing purposes of their own as a constant variable, so it's difficult to tell the difference. Since pre-employment tests only test for the five main drugs (cocaine, marijuana, amphetamines, basic opiates like heroin, and PCP) and other vitamins and minerals that are typically found in urine, it would most likely pass as real urine. They do not test for gender or dig deeper than they need to, because that would cost the lab and employer more money. *But I bet using stinky cat pee would raise a flag.*

I didn't see exactly what the tech wrote down after the heat test, but she bagged the sample up and said she would send it to the lab and told me I should get the results in the next day or two. I left there feeling so nervous and anxious I could not eat for the rest of the day. I went straight to bed to overcome my nerves. During my slumber, I had a vivid dream that a lab tech marked my sample as negative—as in no drugs found.

I got an e-mail the next day from the employer. I quickly opened it, just like you would pull off a Band-Aid. I had passed the test! They wanted me to complete my paper work and start in a week and a half!

The risks and anxiety associated with the experience made me realize I never want to put myself in that situation again. I also want to be clear that I am not recommending that you cheat the system or follow in my footsteps. I also claim no guarantees. I do feel that drug testing for marijuana for many jobs is unwarranted, especially now given the changes in state laws toward legalization in some form. I know that my thoughts on marijuana use do not justify my actions, but sometimes you get put in positions that result in you making suspect choices.

In the end, I worked my butt off for that employer… while the job lasted.

Chapter 11

The Daily Deal Downfall

*Note: You could use this chapter as a drinking game. Take a sip any time I use the word "business" or "deal." That should take some of the edge off from some of these distressing stories. If you want to use the whole book and drink every time I use "unemployed," please don't sue me when you end up getting your stomach pumped.

Mid-year 2011, after quitting the scammy product pushing job and watching my bank account almost hit zero because of several months of unemployment, I was hired by a start-up company which I will refer to as "Enkindle." It existed under an umbrella of a larger company, which focused on rebates and reward programs. Starting a daily deal company seemed like a natural venture for the parent company.

Enkindle, a Groupon copycat, sold group buying coupons. Here's the gist: buy a deal to a spa, restaurant, or activity, and save 50 to 80 off the original price! People were going crazy buying these deals when the concept first hit the scene in 2008. Spend $20 to get $40 worth of Italian cuisine, or $40 for an $80 massage. To bust up a junk car with bats only costs $20 for an hour, a $40 value. For $3 a man will come draw a portrait of your cat, a $15 value! People love these deals because we feel like we are saving money *and* participating in new adventures! In a time when money is tight, getting out of the house and having a good time needs to be affordable, and these deals made it possible.

The popularity of these sites skyrocketed in the recession years, and soon it seemed that daily deal companies were everywhere. Deal companies were bringing in the best restaurants and experiences and offering them to customers at absurdly discounted prices. People were ecstatic to be able to save so much money. Business owners were happy to gain business without paying direct out of pocket costs to advertise.

Working for a start-up company can be a risk—especially when the company is late to the game. There was fierce competition in the daily deals space, and I was working for a little fish in a big pond. I was hired with a group of six other recent college graduates to do sales in a role called "'Area Manager." Our job was to call business owners and managers, set up in-person appointments, and basically convince them to discount their products for the public in hopes that this would lead to them getting repeat customers.

On Mondays, everyone in the Area Manager role had to call, call, call; call all day to get as many appointments as possible in our territories. If you have ever done cold calling, you know how draining it can be. People are mean to sales people. They don't care who you are. They don't care what you want. Their main instinct is to say no. But in sales, you are taught that the more *no*'s you get, the closer you are getting to a *yes*. Sometimes we got so frustrated it hurt. Other times, hilarious moments would happen, and we couldn't help but laugh and laugh. My favorite moment was when one member of the team, Jon, phoned a place called The Pretty Kitty. Jon did not know what kind of business it was when he called. We had a certain number of calls to make, so sometimes we didn't have time to do research. We just had to wing it.

Jon: "Hello! Is this the owner of the... uh... The Pretty Kitty?"
Woman: "Yes..."
Jon: "I'd like to talk to you about how we can increase awareness of your business. Do you have a moment to discuss getting more people to come to your Pretty Kitty business?"

Moments later, he found out it was a bikini waxing salon. *Oh the euphemisms!*

After call day, we spent the rest of the week driving around in our own cars to meet with potential clients. I didn't even have my own car at this point, as my old one broke down from age and all the driving I had done at my scammy product pushing job.[xvi] I was driving around in my mom's

---

[xvi] We will discuss this in the last chapter!

Jeep until I could save up to buy a new car of my own. At this point in my life, company cars felt like a myth to me, like the existence of jackalopes.

Business owners thought the daily deal was a great idea in the beginning. They only had to pay per performance, meaning, they only owed money based on what deals sold; they owed no money up front. The goal was for the new customer to come in and try their product or service at a discounted rate. Hopefully patrons would have such a good experience they would come back again and pay full price. It *seemed* like a savvy way to boost business. Enkindle was a late bloomer, so some businesses that had already tried the daily deal once or twice were skeptical. Others were desperate and willing to do anything to get a client in the door.

The problem with these deals, after few years into the scene, was that many consumers started to expect that they would never have to pay full price for anything. They got so used to their discounts that they knew they could just wait for the next site to pop up with a similar deal, or they would just deal-hop all the places in their neighborhoods… or even travel an hour away… just to save 70 percent. And with only a 50/50 or 60/40 split paid back to the business, business owners were losing more money than they'd expected. Let's do some math together: [xvii] $10 for $20 on a deal sold to the customer, with a 50/50 split on the actual selling price of the deal between the business and the deal company = $5 back to the business. So they get back $5 back for the selling price of $20 worth of food, products, tickets, or services. Now, in some extreme cases, some restaurants would

---

[xvii] I can't believe I just said that! Let's just say math is not my favorite subject.

sell 50,000 of these $10 for $20 deals! That's $1 million worth of food, and they were only making $250,000 back. That's essentially a $750,000 marketing campaign!

Apparently, the best deal that Groupon ever sold was $25 for $50 worth of clothing at Nordstrom Rack in November 2010. I remember this deal because I worked for said company when this deal was available. I had never heard of Groupon at the time. All the employees were shocked by the madhouse it created. The line stretched out the door. And what a pain it was to have to enter in all these coupons manually rather than just scanning the deal like a regular coupon, or like we do ever so effortlessly from our phones now! Roughly 623,000 people purchased the coupon, generating a total of $15.6 million or 2.6 percent of Groupon's cumulative revenue in 2010, according to the *Harvard Business Review*. The question is: who actually benefits the most from these deals? The deal site, provider, or buyer?

There was no telling how many people would buy any given deal. Sure, businesses could put a limit on the number of deals available. But even so, it was sometimes so hard to manage the crowds that would show up for a deal, so businesses were not able to give the customers great service. And when the first experience is not great, it leaves little hope for repeat business. At first, business owners were happy to sign up, but as more and more of them became savvier, they realized that the daily deals marketing model was not usually in the best interest of the company. They just couldn't afford to lose those margins.

After only a few years of this marketing phenomenon, the majority of deals that one could find—other than on Groupon—were service deals, for which businesses would essentially inflate the original cost. They knew that people wanted steep deals, but they had to embellish how much their services were usually worth just so their deals could seem deeply discounted to compete with the rest of the market.

Over the course of a few years, the daily deal companies began to die off. They just could not compete with Groupon. Even Groupon would have to figure out how to hold steady to stay in the game, with its stock taking a tumble. Investors and merchants began to question the longevity of such a business model. And people stopped buying as many deals because the ones that were available were the same, boring deals. Gone was the abundance of good food and activity deals. Left were the carpet cleaning and haircut deals that you could get every day. The thrill of the limited-time offer died. The fear of missing out was gone, because consumers knew they could find the deal again. Businesses knew better than to try to appeal to what they called "bargain hunters" or "coupon cutters." Some merchants told me that running a daily deal had been one of the worst decisions they'd ever made.

Enkindle was no exception to the general trend. Our problem was not over-selling deals. Our problem was that we couldn't get enough buys because no one knew about us! About a month after our party of six sales reps were hired, Enkindle made huge layoffs, and half the employees were let go without warning. They even fired our sales manager and one of our underperforming sales reps. *Poor Jon.* Then there were only five of us sales reps. Three of my team members got smart and found new jobs shortly after that. And then there were two. Trey and I quickly became buddies and would talk about all of the flaws of the company's business model. He tried to make it work for a while, but in the end, he quit too, and I was the only salesperson left. I later learned that the only reason Trey stayed at the job for so long was because his mom was the Director of HR at the parent company!

Even with the struggles, the investors kept the company going. It was like they had a never-ending supply of money that was wasted on developing new ways to sell the deals. Sure, I was bringing in four to five deals a week from businesses, but what did that mean if no consumers saw the carefully constructed discount? Our viewership just was not there. Enkindle did not spend enough time marketing the brand, and spent too much time worrying about gathering as many deals as possible.

After losing the rest of my team, I was given a new role as an Account Manager. I was pulled in from doing outside sales after I had spent about eight months in the field, because the bosses had decided to try a new strategy: multi-level marketing. A stigma exists around this strategy, as if all multi-level marketing is some sort of Ponzi scheme. What our baby deal company decided to do was to offer all of our collected deals in an online database, for a small fee, to customers who wanted to make money by selling the deals directly to their friends, families and social networks. For every deal they sold, they would get a percentage of commission. The thought was that people would much rather hear of a business by word of mouth from a trusted friend, and then —boom!—be offered a great deal by them.

My job at this point was to partner with "mommy bloggers" and "coupon-savvy influencers" who would get a percentage of the profit to help us market our deals. Initially, getting people on board did not take much convincing. I was offering up what seemed like an easy way to make side cash. But behind the scenes was a tizzy of issues. What we had left in the database were not exactly deals people wanted. Some businesses would fold and not tell us, resulting in deals that were obsolete. A dire problem was that we were asking people who didn't work for the company to donate all this extra time to promoting and selling our deals, and it wasn't working. You can't ask someone who isn't a full employee to do full-time work. The deals still were not selling well, and I was under a lot of pressure to help make a business model work that I didn't agree with in the first place.

The new scheme seemed extremely flawed to me. What if some of the deals we had never made it in front of the public? What about the businesses expecting to be advertised that were not being picked by these "deal promoters?" Why were we not promoting our own brand name more? We were not bringing in any new deals anymore, and as many as ten deals a day were marked as expired due to businesses closing or owners backing out, saying we were not delivering what we had promised. It was like the investors were just trying to see what kind of money they could make off of the lackluster deals that were left. All the signs of failure were there, yet

Enkindle pushed on and tried to hide from the employees that there was crummy news in our future.

At this point there were four of us in account management, as well as a small team of tech developers. Most of us were young and new in our careers. I didn't have an opportunity to get to know the account managers before, since I had spent so much time either on the phone or in the field doing sales. After I was switched to full-time in the office, I got pretty close to one of the account managers, Jessica. She and I would often find ourselves with nothing to do. For a company that was supposedly trying to work its butt off to save itself, the lower-level employees were left with nothing but busy work. Jess and I would go outside on the patio and talk about the decisions Enkindle made, and wonder how it was still afloat. We decided the only reason we were still in business must be because we had rich investors from our parent company.

That's when Jessica and I started to become suspicious. We knew the sales numbers. We knew at this point that almost everyone in the company had either been laid off or quit. We would see people from HR and the sales leaders go into private meetings together. We overheard talks of a "Plan C." But I didn't have anywhere to go; I had not found a new job yet. I was stuck in a company that was about to go under and everyone above us was trying to keep it from us, as if we were ignorant. We had gone from being in a high-stress, demanding work environment where we were always busy, to having barely any work to do.

We began to question everything, discussing the signs of impending doom, and how these people were delusional for thinking they could save the company. *Godspeed for trying!* We would scurry like curious cats around the office trying to see what the bosses were up to. We would chatter about what we thought they were saying behind closed doors. We would pretend we were detectives trying to figure out clues to what was next. *Who would be the first to admit to company murder?* This ridiculousness is what happens when companies are not transparent with their employees.

We talked about how we didn't have much time left. But the weeks turned into months, and for some reason we all still had "jobs." We joked about how we wished they would just let us go, already. There are only so many fashion ideas and funny memes you can pin on Pinterest in one day. There are only so many ways you can organize your cubicle. There are only so many shoe sites you can look at before you drive yourself insane. There are only so many jobs you can apply to in one day in a wishy-washy economy, and I wasn't having luck landing interviews. Jessica had already read several books in a few short months because there was so little to do. Now, I don't want to be one to complain about not having to work hard for my money. Sure, a little downtime is great, but for me, it wasn't fulfilling. I wasn't learning or growing. I was stagnating. It was like being stuck in a bad relationship, waiting for the other person to just break up with you so you get all the benefits of the breakup *and* all the sympathy for being dumped. We were sitting ducks just hanging out in our cubicles waiting for a shot to be fired.

As time went on, I would drive by places that I had previously signed up to run a deal, and see that just a short few months later many would have "Out Of Business" signs plastered on the windows. People all over were making questionable business decisions that weren't working in their favor. The businesses couldn't survive in the tough economy, and neither could the company trying to advertise for them. The whole daily deals environment was unstable. Plus, the competition from the large deal companies made it laborious to stay afloat.

When the end finally came, the four of us left on the accounts side of the company were called into our boss's office. He finally told us what we had known was coming: Enkindle would cease to exist, and we would be put on unemployment benefits.

At first I felt relieved to be done with yet another bust of a job. But it was discouraging. Just 11 months before, I had started my first day at Enkindle. But here I was again, re-entering the unemployment line—and for the first time, legally being recognized as unemployed by the government. The only positive for me was that at least the unemployment money would help alleviate some of the stress of paying bills. But I began to wonder what would come next for me. Were there any stable jobs for young professionals in this weakened economy?

Chapter 12

Baiting The Unemployed

"A baited cat may grow as fierce as a lion."

Samuel Palmer

I have only been deemed eligible for unemployment benefits once in my life, when the daily deals company I worked for went belly-up. For a slight moment, it seemed like a relief to be deemed "professionally unemployed" with a steady paycheck coming in! Granted, I lived at home, and if I had been paying rent, the benefits would not have covered that expense. I was just grateful I did not have to tap too much into my savings account to get by. It helped alleviate some of the stress of losing my job. But official unemployment comes with many caveats and complications.

The paperwork that comes with unemployment is extensive. You are paid based on factors such as how you became unemployed, what your wages were at your last job, the number of hours you worked, and how long you were with the company. You are granted a set amount of time to receive money, or a set allowance. Once the allowance is gone, you cannot receive any more aid. I was granted around six months of unemployment after being laid off from the daily deals company. I was issued a reloadable debit card for expenses.

To be eligible for unemployment, you must be "actively looking for a job." The government has its ways to verify whether you are actually putting yourself out there. Sure, there are ways to cheat the system, but you can be penalized at a felony level, so I don't advise trying anything like that! You must also have been laid off from your job; you cannot quit. In many cases you cannot have been fired. State law determines whether a fired employee can collect unemployment. Generally speaking, an employee who is fired for serious misconduct is ineligible for benefits, either entirely or at least for a certain period of time.

People who receive unemployment checks often get a bad rep. While some people do understand and have sympathy for those not working, just as many people are quick to point out how those collecting unemployment are simply enjoying "funemployment" while leeching off of all of those who still have jobs. But research suggests that is very much untrue. A study done by Congress' Joint Economic Committee found that beneficiaries of unemployment benefits actually spend more time actively searching for work than those who are ineligible for the benefits.[56] This makes sense: those receiving unemployment benefits work harder to find jobs because receiving benefits is dependent on recipients looking for work—and proving it.

The process of receiving my unemployment benefits in 2012 started with filling out paperwork with the company that laid me off, and then with the Texas Workforce Commission. Every week I had to check into the TWC website and fill out a form proving that I had applied to at least five jobs that week. I had to report how many estimated hours I'd spent looking for work. I also had to report when I went out of town, worked any side jobs, had any interviews, went to any job fairs, or had any job offers. One week I went to Austin and claimed it as time out of town on my report. So guess what? They did not pay me for that week. They also made me log in to certain job sites every week, and would track my activity to see if I was actually looking around on the site. If not, they would question my job searching status. Being monitored so closely didn't help my morale when looking for work, and it often felt like a lot of busy work.

Another daunting fact about unemployment is that those who experience long term unemployment are less likely to get hired.[57] Potential employers look closely at how long you were at a previous job, or whether you have been unemployed for a long period of time. If you are with a company for less than a year or unemployed for more than six months, you will most likely be judged for it and asked about it by potential employers in interviews.

A candidate who is a job-hopper raises a red flag to employers, but sometimes the candidate's work history reflects the fact that they have not been able to catch a break. Changing jobs is also a key way for workers to make more money. That's especially true for younger workers who often need to move around to find jobs that suit and pay us best. By entering the workforce during a period of prolonged economic downturn, young people miss out on years of potential wage gains, and often have to look for new opportunities to get a decent raise.

I had to explain over and over again in interviews why I had gone through so many jobs. I was viewed as a non-committal job-hopper, but really, I had just not found the right job for me yet! I wanted to be able to feel accomplished in my work. I was just having a string of bad luck.

If being unemployed isn't bad enough, you have other circumstances to worry about that come with the official status. You have to be careful to avoid unemployment scams. It seems like scams are always out to get you when you are most vulnerable. If you are naive or just do not know what you are doing, you could become a victim of the heartless people who prey on people receiving benefits. When you are out of work you can be vulnerable or desperate for money, making you a prime target.

I once received a check for $1,000 in the mail, with instructions to "mystery shop" my customer experience at a Western Union. The instructions stated I first would need to deposit the check into my bank account, keep $300 for myself as payment, then go to a Western Union to wire the rest of the money to a specified third party, then fill out a customer experience evaluation form. *Umm... What!?* Sure, someone could have fallen for it, but thankfully, to me it raised a red flag. The official-looking check was bogus. My bank would probably have taken it, believing it to be good. Then, after I'd wired the $700 to the third party and the bank found out the check hadn't cleared, I would have been on the hook for paying back all the money. I wondered how these people knew my address. It turns out scams like this happen across the nation. Scammers target people who post their resumes and addresses on job boards.

I found through online searches that people run e-mail scams by sending messages attempting to get unemployment debit card information, or other personal information from people receiving benefits, so they can steal their money or use the information for identity theft. Some websites state offers to file for unemployment benefits or extended unemployment benefits for a fee to expedite the process for you. It is important to know that *you* are the only person who can apply online for unemployment benefits, and you have to file directly on your state unemployment office website. Third parties cannot file for unemployment benefits for you. If you get a phone call asking for your unemployment debit card information or other personal information regarding your unemployment claim, it's a scam. Unemployment scams can be reported to the Internet Crime Complaint Center, The Federal

Trade Commission, and the Better Business Bureau. Even Google will look into illegitimate websites.

Finally, after months of diligently searching, I was hired by a Dallas dating site to sell memberships to people. The job had the potential to be lucrative, and it sounded interesting. Who was I to judge people for trying to find love online? I myself have formed some friendships and relationships online. I also have friends who have gone on to get married, and even have kids, partly because of a little common denominator... me! *I'm a naked baby with wings!*[xviii]

The manager of the dating site told me I would only be consulting with people who had registered on the site and had expressed interest in becoming a member. He gushed at how exciting it is to talk to people about what they were looking for in a spouse. The membership would provide them a real matchmaker that would help find them dates in the pool of existing members. I learned that this dating site gave discounts or free memberships to white women between the ages of 21-25, or to affluent black men, because of the high demand for these demographics. For others, memberships at this company started at $2,500 a year!

[xviii] Cupid, the classic matchmaker.

I was hired at the same time as two other women who, I learned from our conversations, were so desperate for cash that they would have taken any job. I felt for them, as I was sort of in the same boat. We all thought it sounded like a fun job to just talk to regular people and help them find love.

But we had been misled. It was a classic bait and switch; being hired for one job, only to learn that the daily work would be totally different. I thought I had been hired to sell memberships. Instead, after taking the handbook test and acing it, I was shown what we would actually be doing.

On the third day of training (which, I might add, was the 4th of July—weekends and holidays were required), I met the team of women I would be working with. Some looked angry and worn out as they sat their desks all lined up in a small room with an open floor plan. It was an odd group and the aura of the room was gray. A brunette that looked like an MMA fighter mentioned how she had earned the most comfortable chair in the room by being at the company the longest, and that if anyone tried to take it she would surely start a cat fight. One large gal kept on dipping chips in some sort of artificial crab slaw goop, and constantly talked with her mouth full of food. One girl wearing an extremely short dress cautioned me to never to use my cell phone during work hours because it would be taken away.

The real job turned out to consist solely of calling people, who had entered their information on the company site, to convince them to come into the office for a meeting. I would not be meeting people in person. I would be required to wear a headset all day while the automatic phone system dialed numbers for me, and when someone picked up, I was supposed to read off a script. I was to ask personal questions to weed out the people who were not a good fit, like the unemployed, janitors, people who had been to jail, most black women, people over 60 (yes, they discriminated to the fullest extent), and fight to lure "good" people into the office to be pitched on an expensive membership. Once a person signed a membership contract, I learned it was nearly impossible to get out of it until it expired. I also learned that the job pay was nowhere near the advertised $50,000 plus a year. It was commission based. The whole set up, the script, and the people in the room just made me feel uneasy. Worst of all, I was missing out on 4th of July fun just to bother people on their holiday!

I was told that the company kept every single name and phone number in the system forever. They explained they would keep calling these people over and over again if they did not pick up, or if they just answered and hung up. No matter how many times people explicitly said they were not interested, the company would continue calling them. I learned companies even have specific phrases that must be said to actually take a person off a call list; just saying "take me off your list" may not be good enough. For this company, saying you got married would work to get you off the list. I learned that companies will call you as many times as they legally can just to try to make a sale. That first day, I heard a woman on the other end of the phone threaten to get lawyers involved because she was sick of the endless phone calls. *What kind of business were they running here?* Not only had I been misled, but they were treating potential customers poorly. *This was not for me!* I asked to be let go early, since it was a holiday and all. I never returned and I never got paid for my three days of training. I was okay with that, because it meant I did not have to claim work on my unemployment forms.

The bait and switch can happen to anyone, but in a hostile job market where Millennials are constantly on the lookout for good opportunities, this type of recruiting is easy. Companies are constantly flooded with job applications from a large pool of talented Millennials who are already underpaid, unemployed, or working part-time. They know that advertising with a juicy fish will lure in the cats. *Here, kitty, kitty! Come and get it!* But sometimes, that fish is full of mercury, sharp bones, or worms.

If you ever feel an employer is being misleading about what kind of job you are interviewing for, it's important to try to clarify the situation and then decide whether to accept the job based on the information you get. Before you sign a contract or agree to the job, you should make sure you get the terms of the agreement and the position's responsibilities in writing to ensure no additional surprises.

I continued to receive my unemployment benefits and was doing my best to keep applying, networking, going to job fairs and taking lengthy calls with recruiters. I was even called in to my local unemployment office where I had to sit through a mandatory two-hour meeting with about 20 other people to learn how to best utilize my time, and how to use the tools offered by the state to aid me in finding a good job as quickly possible.

I learned that it's not about taking the first job available, unless you absolutely must! In the end, it's about doing research and making sure a job is going to give you the experience and the respect that a hard worker deserves. How did I keep ending up in companies that were not what they seemed? Employers can be very good at tricking people into thinking that a job is something that it is not. I learned not to be a lamb in interviews anymore. I had to be a lion, and go in with hard-hitting questions so as not to fall into the traps that are everywhere when you are desperately looking for work. Remember, interviewers are not the only ones allowed to be inquisitive.

In a world where good jobs are tough to get, it's not always easy to be picky. But from experience, I learned that the jobs that give you that gut feeling of "no" usually don't pan out, or you end up getting burned out fast. You can take a job to pay the bills, but don't start a career based on iffy feelings. You won't be happy. Money comes and goes, but mental well-being is more important than some job.

Chapter 13

Wage Rage!

Does it make sense to work for cents?

Working for just above minimum wage gave me a personal look at the harsh reality that millions of Americans face every day, trying to simply survive on low wages. During Obama's term, the White House made a push to increase the national minimum wage from $7.25 an hour to $10.10 an hour, but it remained unchanged when he left office. The minimum wage has in no way kept up with inflation and does not provide what is considered a livable income to an individual, and by no means is enough to support a family. In a world where job creation of higher paying jobs is lacking, working low wage jobs is the only option many people have.

When I earned $10 an hour working in retail as a college graduate, I was lucky enough to be able to live with my parents, eliminating all rent and utility costs. At 40 hours a week, before taxes, that's $1,600 a month, or $19,200 a year. With taxes taken out, I took home $1,476 a month, or $17,712 per year. Once you factor in paying for transportation to get to work, a cell phone, food and supplies, health care, and student loans, it is safe to say that not much is left. For most individuals, that is not enough to afford a roof over their heads. How can anyone be expected to be financially independent and contribute to a savings account on $10 an hour? Now, lower that number to $7.25 an hour, the actual minimum wage we've had in this country since 2009. [xix]

Economists say that since 1968, if the minimum wage had been tied to inflation, the pay rate would be $10.52 an hour. If it had been tied to productivity, it would be $21.72.[58] Everything has gone up in price: school, housing, groceries; yet wages have not increased to keep up. With an income of $15,080 a year before taxes, it is hard for a person making minimum wage to get by. Yet, the Census Bureau reports 30 percent of America's workforce earns a near-minimum-wage salary—that's almost 21 million people. More than 45 million people, or 14.5 percent of all Americans, live below the poverty line.[59]

Minimum wage jobs have traditionally been beginner jobs that pushed people to move up the ladder or eventually learn more skills and move on to higher-paying jobs. Perceptions are that these jobs are for pimple-faced

---

[xix] For further reading about the reality of low-wage workers, I recommend Barbara Ehrenreich's *Nickeled and Dimed: On Getting By in America* (Henery Holt and Company, 2001), in which a PhD-holding journalist goes undercover in three major American cities and lives on minimum wage. The book details how difficult it was just to survive. Though the book is nearly 20 years old, the situation it reveals is largely unchanged.

kids or those who are simply unmotivated. But the reality is the world has changed. More people with college degrees are working for pay that can hardly pay back loans—and I was one of them for a time. In 2013, 260,000 Americans with a bachelor's degree or higher worked for the federal minimum wage or less, which was nearly 120,000 *more* people than a decade prior, according to data from the Bureau of Labor Statistics. The number of Americans with at least a bachelor's degree making minimum wage has dropped from its post-recession high watermark (327,000 in 2010), but it's still much higher than it was before the economy bottomed out (127,000 in both 2005 and 2006). Another 200,000 associate degree holders also worked for minimum wage in 2013.

No college graduate goes to school, pays all that money and invests all that time to live near poverty. Isn't that the whole point of going to college—to make more than minimum wage? To not have to live paycheck to paycheck?

We can't pussy foot around the real problem: enough jobs do not exist... that people see as a life-long career! Young people are out of work, just as folks from every other age group are out of work. Why does it seem like a majority of the jobs available are arguably thankless, low paying jobs? According to a recent analysis by the National Employment Law Project (NELP), the biggest growth in private-sector job creation after the recession occurred were in positions in the low-wage retail, administrative, and food service sectors of the economy. While 23 percent of the jobs lost in the Great Recession that followed the economic meltdown of 2008 were "low-wage" (those paying $9-$13 an hour), 49 percent of new jobs added during the sluggish "recovery" are in those same low-wage industries. On the other end of the spectrum, 40 percent of the jobs lost were higher paying ($19-$31 an hour), while a mere 14 percent of new jobs pay similarly high wages.[60]

No one is entitled to any pay. If you want higher pay, yes, get an education. But even then, how will you pay for said education without taking out major loans? How can you be sure you will be making more than someone at Walmart? In today's world, educated people are forced into low-paying jobs simply because better jobs are not always readily available. It's what experts call "cyclical downgrade." The problem is a systematic destruction of jobs that pay middle-class wages. These jobs are being replaced with "lower-rung," "low-mobility" jobs. While some argue it is a lack of "skills enhancement" that keeps the wage market-rate low for these jobs, it's sometimes all that's available to millions of people, including college graduates.

The subject of raising the minimum wage sparks fierce debate. Arguments for raising the minimum wage include that it will provide more people a decent living wage so we will be able to buy more, thus stimulating the economy. It would also reduce the expense of social programs. It would create a decrease in employee turnover rates, meaning that the more people make, the happier we are at jobs, and the more likely we are to stay and put in hard work. Many economic surveys have found that raises can increase morale, productivity, performance, enhance customer service, reduce employee turnover, and attract better, smarter job candidates. Companies may find it in their best interest to set their own fair wages. Paying someone the bare minimum will only buy minimum skills and effort. According to a 2014 Congressional Budget Office (CBO) study, raising the minimum wage would bring 900,000 people out of poverty, almost 25 million people would see an increase in wages, but an unknown number (estimated 500,000 people) would lose jobs.[61]

Arguments against raising the minimum wage say it will create job layoffs, as businesses will not be able to afford to hold on to employees, and that competition for certain jobs will go up as employers will expect more out of their employees if they are paying out higher wages. Some argue a higher minimum wage will make it that much harder for young people to get starter jobs, which will impact the ability to gain experience. It is easier said than done to provide people an income to survive on. Large businesses like McDonalds and Walmart can afford to pay people a better working wage and still make billions in profit, but some small businesses may not be able to support an increase in payroll expenses. In consumer economies and capitalist societies, businesses tend to react to minimum wage increases by raising the prices of the goods and services they provide. *Oh pickles! The price of a Big Mac will be too much!* But most commodities over the years have already gone up in costs, and base pay has not followed suit.

Raising the minimum wage is tricky, because it needs to be a rate that keeps pace with inflation, but not so high a rate that it causes too much inflation of the cost of products or services. If minimum wages rise, then naturally, all other wages could, and arguably should, go up as well.

Many argue the case that the minimum wage should be a living wage, but it is hard to tell just what the right formula is. Do we raise the minimum wage for certain ages, like those over 18 or 21? For only certain types of jobs or companies? Do we do away with the minimum wage altogether, and let the market dictate prices? All the while, the current system is costing the average taxpayer money because of the subsidies many of these low-wage workers receive from the government.

On the opposite spectrum, since 1978, CEO pay at American firms has risen 725 percent, which is more than 127 times faster than worker pay over the same time period, according to data from the Economic Policy Institute. From 1978 to 2011, CEO compensation increased at a rate substantially greater than stock market growth and the painfully slow 5.7 percent growth in worker compensation.[xx] And shows like *Undercover Boss* only prove the fact that many CEOs are not fully aware how their businesses operate from the bottom rung, or understand the struggles caused by low pay rates. Why are CEOs being rewarded at a level that doesn't seem to be commensurate to their contributions to their organizations, especially in cases where they are running failing organizations?

It can be argued that corporations exist to make money, not to provide for society. But the "Deloitte Millennial Survey 2016" revealed that 90

[xx] You can just picture the fat cats with slabs of tuna on their bellies surrounded by unnecessarily lavish toys saying, "Oh, the minimum wage is fine, but don't mess with the maximum wage!"

percent of this generation globally believes that "the success of a business should be measured in terms of more than just its financial performance."⁶² We want businesses to serve a cause or purpose, too. So, shouldn't we do what we can to help our fellow human beings and not just make people at the top of the corporate ladder wealthier?

Desperation for money is a huge motivator for survival and can lead people to make questionable decisions. *Like when your hourly pay rate can't even buy you an entrée dinner at the same restaurant you work at, so you sit there licking your chops, waiting for the person to finish their plate so you can scrounge up that leftover shrimp.* But in all seriousness, when we are in desperate need of money, we can trick ourselves into making decisions that are not viable, but seem to be our only hope in a world where the price for things is ever-increasing and pay rates remain stagnant. They say life is, by definition, survival. But isn't life about much more than that? About more than just figuring out a way to get by? Money doesn't buy happiness, but it supplies a sense of freedom.

We hear stories, we know people, or we ourselves have made decisions based on desperation. Many illegal deeds are done with good intentions lurking close behind: The college student who sells weed to help pay for books and tuition. The young man from a broken home who holds up a woman at an ATM to get money to feed his younger siblings. The woman who uses the Internet to sell her body to help pay her rent. The struggling cashier who works three jobs and still feels the need to pocket small bills from the cash register. The socially awkward person who doesn't do well in interviews and so hides behind the computer to catfish people out of money and goods. The person who can't afford their minor surgery, so he sells his prescription pain pills to help pay his medical bills. The boy who joins a gang because he is angry at the way his social class lacks opportunities for advancement. Tight finances lead to a complicated life.

With social problems such as high unemployment, low wages, increasing college costs, and expensive health care, is our economy contributing to the creation of more desperate criminals? Are we living in a society where people undermine the law because they feel the law does not necessarily have their best interests in mind?

How can we create better opportunity?

We can howl and hiss over what should be done, but in the end, raising the minimum wage does not create jobs or solve poverty and the complicated issues that come with it. The solution is not to continue to create low paying jobs, but to create more skilled jobs and provide the affordable education needed to allow people to provide for themselves and their families. We need to inform people of the types of jobs that America is trying to fill, and make it easier for people to become educated to perform those roles. As referenced before in my chapter "The Disconnects," we need to do a better job linking what we learn in school to real world applications. We also need to look to the future and hypothesize what kind of jobs will be needed in technology, renewable energy, infrastructure, and how people will obtain information and goods in the coming years. Job creation is a fundamental way out of our current high levels of unemployment and low level jobs.

Many Millennials also have the ideas and innovative qualities of successful entrepreneurs. With more guidance, funding, and encouragement, this entrepreneurial spirit might just run free and do its part in creating more jobs and rescuing the economy. Millennials say the ability to get a loan or credit is the biggest challenge to starting a business, with almost two-thirds saying that we do not receive enough support from banks.[63] Another obstacle is the lack of education and resources needed to run a small business, which could be better addressed by high schools and colleges. Millennials would like to see Congress and experienced business tycoons work together to make it easier for people to start a business by providing increased access to education, training, mentors and student loan relief. Though starting a business or inventing a product or service is hard work, for many of us capable Millennials, being our own bosses and helping create the future sounds like just what we need to fix the crisis. Success is not guaranteed, but we have to try. That means that many of us Millennials need to dig down deep and start thinking of ways we can start new businesses and create jobs. This also means those who are already successful need to pay it forward by means of knowledge and resources.

We also need to fight for policy makers to start making decisions in the interest of boosting America's workforce. We need to promote a culture of freedom and innovation in America. We need to simplify burdensome processes that create roadblocks and increase the cost of doing business, which is a barrier to entry for many beginning and growing businesses. We need to offer tax credits to investors who help back startups. We need to teach entrepreneurship in our school systems and encourage the applied learning of science, engineering, math, and technical skills.

Regulation hits small businesses the hardest. Small businesses cannot afford the legal and consultant teams used by big businesses to navigate complex regulations. The Small Business Administration Office of Advocacy found that small businesses face 36 percent higher regulatory costs per employee than large businesses. Small business creates two out of every three new jobs, so excessive burdens on these businesses have a trickle-down effect. By paying too much just to exist, it makes it hard for businesses to even consider raising wages.

We, the people, also need to support small businesses. If we ourselves are not even supporting small businesses, how can we expect them to thrive? It's unsettling to know that certain big box retailers make billions and dominate the U.S. workspace and economy, while individuals working to make their own businesses grow are struggling. America used to be built on small business, but large corporations have taken over and forced many local shops to shut their doors.

The bottom line is that supporting small business, promoting entrepreneurship, creating good jobs with decent wages, and preparing people for the new jobs that come with the ever-changing job market is paramount to our nation's recovery.

Chapter 14

Broke And Broken

Being unemployed or underemployed, facing an unpredictable future, and dealing with money problems can add strife to any relationship. As I progressed through my twenties, I experienced firsthand how not having a job or a plan can be a burden and have damaging effects on relationships.

Throughout my time at university, and for some time after, I had a steady boyfriend. Let's call him Larry. We were together for four-and-a-half years. That's a long time for a person in their early twenties to live, love, and grow with someone. We met at a mutual friend's party and went through all the trials and tribulations of college together. Being in a long-term relationship during college can be a whirlwind of emotions. On one hand, you don't have to deal with many real-world issues as most of your free time together involves partying, studying, or spending time in bed, binge watching *Buffy the Vampire Slayer*. On the other hand, you are still so young, and the only constant in your life is change. It can be challenging to grow together while still trying to figure out who you are individually and what you want after college.

The first summer as a college graduate came and went, and I still did not have a full-time job. I was running out of money, and yearned for some stability. Larry, unaware of the bigger economic picture and harsh realities of the job market, delayed entry into the real world with his plans to earn an MBA at Wisconsin. He has big dreams of working for a fortune 500 company. I wasn't exactly sure of my goals; I just wanted to be happy.

Before Larry left for grad school, he picked arguments with me about the future and my goals. He worried that if we got married, I would just rely on him and his money to survive. He feared I was not ambitious enough. I promised him that was not the case.

For a long-distance relationship, daily life was going okay. I worked a full-time job in retail and he studied full-time. We did not see much of each other, but when we did, it was fun and we made each other laugh. We had our moments when we would bicker, and went through some passion ruts, but I told myself that was natural for people who had been together for years or were struggling through hard times.

In the winter of 2010, after he'd been away at grad school for one semester, Larry asked my dad for my hand in marriage. He said that his time away from me had not changed his love for me. He saw how hard I was working toward bettering myself (doing my best to earn commissions by slinging products in bulk-buying clubs) and said he wanted to give us a chance for the long haul. He proposed to me in my parent's kitchen, in front of my family, and I said yes! We spent the night eating and drinking at a lovely 5-star hotel. I couldn't believe that I was engaged at such a young age. I couldn't believe that I was going to be someone's wife, before I even figured out my career.

A few months into our engagement, after a night of lying on my floor thinking about my life and watching the ceiling fan turn in circles and gather dust, I went to sleep feeling addled. During my slumber I dreamed that I caught my fiancé kissing another girl at a party, so we ended our relationship, and I broke away from our sad little conversation by jumping off a balcony into a pool. I woke up in a panic, sweating as though I really had taken a dip in water. The heart-shaped diamond necklace he had given me for graduation had broken off my neck. I stared at the delicate white gold chain and then twiddled my calla lily cut engagement ring, wondering what it all meant.

When I called him the next day he seemed distant, and when I asked him if he loved me, he said in a hostile tone, *"I am marrying you, aren't I?"*

Time went on and I still could not get out of retail. I thought about moving with my fiancé to Florida, just for the summer, so I could be with him as he did his internship. He constantly expressed concern that I didn't have enough going on in my life other than him. We often would fight over the fact that I was underemployed. Larry would send me articles and links to jobs all the time, encouraging me—nay, nagging me—to find a job. He would ask me too many questions. *"How many people did you send your resume to today? Did you sign up for that networking event? Did you contact that recruiter? Did you see the link I sent you today of new job I found? You have all the time in the world, why didn't you get it done?"*

He didn't understand that is wasn't so easy. He didn't understand how hard it was to find a decent job in a saturated market. He came from a privileged family and was in the graduate school bubble, so he had no idea what it was like to be in my shoes. It was like he didn't try to understand. I thought he knew me better. I thought he knew that I wanted more for myself than to just be someone's wife. I wanted a life where I could make a name for myself and earn my own money. My fiancé just didn't think I was progressing fast enough, even though I was only 24.

On the eve of his 24th birthday, I told him I was excited he was in town and I was glad we were getting along so well after so much time apart. I was relaxed and happy. I sat on his lap and mentioned how close I felt to him at that moment. It was then that he told me he wanted to break up. Time seemed to stand still for a moment as I struggled to process the words he had just uttered.

I don't know if the distance and time pulled us apart. I don't know if my lack of a steady job frustrated him to the point of no return. I don't know if my broken necklace and dream were real premonitions or just something my subconscious conjured up based on our rough patches. I think it might have been a mix of elements. But my world came crashing down. I hit rock bottom. I had no job, place of my own, or savings. I lost the one person I counted on for stability. Everything I thought I knew drastically changed forever.

I couldn't eat. I didn't sleep for three whole days straight. When I did finally sleep, I woke up with feelings of depression and it was a struggle to get myself out of bed or showered. Every time I thought about him my stomach did summersaults.

But deep down, I knew that it wasn't meant to be. Four-and-a-half years had come and gone, and it was time to move on. I knew I had to snap out of it soon and figure myself out. I had to figure out my own happiness. I could not waste time mulling over the past.

I put all my time and energy into finding, not just any job, but a job that would help me learn and grow—and grow my bank account. About a month after the breakup, I got the job at the daily deal company that included nice commissions and health benefits. I started to feel like a real grown up. I was new to being single, but my friends convinced me that I needed to have a night on the town drinking, dancing, and flirting. I ended up getting a few numbers that summer night. But I couldn't get my mind off the young man who had stopped me randomly just to tell me he thought I was beautiful. I ended up going out with him a few weeks later.

A month or so after that date, the new guy (let's call him Wyatt) and I were entwined in an emotional and physical whirlwind. He wasn't sure he wanted a relationship. I wasn't sure I was ready for one. But we fell for each other fast, fueled by our physical attraction to each other.

Nine months into our relationship, Wyatt got laid off from his job. He decided to pack up and move to Austin, his college town, to live with one of his buddies. I had told myself I would never do long distance again, but love and lust will cause a person do crazy things.

I was making pretty good commissions at my job. He was broke and on unemployment, so I helped feed him and tried to plan fun distractions for when we got together, like time at the pool or cooking new recipes. I watched him struggle with his external and internal demons. His friends and I would often joke that he was a "Negative Nancy," since he mumble grumbled about life a lot, which often sounded more humorous than serious. But I soon realized he was slipping into a state of depression, and he would find ways to temporarily increase his serotonin levels. He was easily distracted from job searching, and tried many times to push me away by saying I deserved someone who had his act together. It took a toll on our relationship. We broke up and got back together many times. It was like a typical Taylor Swift song.

A few months later, the daily deal company I worked for went under and I, too, found myself on unemployment. We stayed together because we felt we needed each other to get through trying times. *Two cute little unemployed kitty cats in a box.* What fun we had, spending all day in bed and exploring Austin at night, cattin' around town. We danced, we drank, we sampled the fare at food trucks, we went floating on the river with friends, and we went to local music shows (where I discovered The Cat Be Unemployed shirt!). We were having a grand time just living the city life. We were not living up to our potential, and we were not a good influence on each other. We indulged each other's laziness and urge to escape reality.

Eventually, after the fun of our relationship wore off, the stress started. Not being able to pay for things became a great concern. Reality hit me when I realized that Wyatt wouldn't move back to Dallas just for me, and it was difficult for me to find a decent job in Austin, as the economy was not as big as Dallas. He pushed me further and further away emotionally, to the point where I felt as though my essence wasn't fully lit. We finally realized how unstable our relationship was and decided to end it *for real*. It had been a long time since I had been truly single, as I had jumped from one serious relationship to another so quickly. After being on and off for nearly two years, we said goodbye.

Here I was, 26-years-old, four years out of school, and I couldn't even keep a job for a whole year. I was starting to feel discouraged, thinking that the only jobs I would ever find were sales jobs. I feared that my relationships would probably continue to suffer because of dissatisfying employment.

During my longest stint of unemployment (six months), there were times where I felt that my working friends did not care about my situation. I felt they were not checking in on me enough. I was lost in an emotional pit. I often felt alone and didn't know how to talk to people about it. I got into spats with my friends and family over irrational matters. I compared my life to other people's on social media, wondering how I had fallen so far behind. I felt like the whole world was against me, and often times it was hard to get out of bed and be motivated.

But it was through being alone and isolated that I learned to become strong. I didn't want to settle anymore. Not in my jobs, and not in my relationships. I was tired of being broke and broken.

My job situations weren't the only cause for my relationships ending, but it did contribute to the relationships falling apart.[xxi] As someone who has been on both sides of the relationship—being the one struggling and being the one watching someone struggle—I learned many lessons about how to handle the delicate situation of being in a relationship while being out of work.

For a relationship to work, it needs passion, intimacy and commitment. Unemployment can attack a relationship from all sides. A person who no longer feels important due to job loss may lose interest in sex, because feeling unsuccessful can correlate to feeling unattractive. The unemployed person may feel like there is little to talk about because a job is no longer a reference point, or that nothing feels as exciting or as interesting as it was

---

[xxi] I sure wasn't perfect in any of these relationships.

before the lack of job. The unemployed person may worry about the doom of a breakup because of job status.

I learned that when your partner is the one unemployed, it's crucial to let your partner know you believe in them. People want to feel loved and supported; it helps keep us motivated. But I also remember that the last thing I wanted was to be nagged about finding a job. It's important to give the unemployed person space, but still check in regularly in a positive way.

I learned the importance of communication, and how to be open and understanding about the situation. If one party is too closed off, or if one party is unwilling to listen to the other, the relationship is bound to go sour. That being said, if the unemployed person is indeed doing nothing to better themselves, then the fault is in their court. A couple has to create goals together. You have to both decide you want to grow together. You must both decide how to balance the future of your career and the progression of the relationship.

For the unemployed, it is important to show your partner you are being proactive. You need to show them you are not just going to throw in the towel. You have to show that you can stay motivated in dire times, no matter how difficult it may be. Your partner may view how hard you work to better yourself as a reflection of how hard you are willing to work at any challenge life throws.

Unemployment itself can cause major health concerns, stress being one of the top contenders. People who are stressed tend to drink or smoke more, or even turn to drugs, which are leading causes of other health or relationship problems. According to physiological studies, unemployed people are twice as likely as their employed counterparts to experience psychological problems such as depression, anxiety, psychosomatic symptoms, low subjective well-being, and poor self-esteem.[64] A Pew Research study found that the unemployed also struggle with a loss of self-respect and the loss of friendships, both of which can increase feelings of isolation and depression and work against the confidence needed to find new work.[65]

Being unemployed challenges you to learn how to make the most of each day. It is important to give meaning to the day and not waste away under the blankets. I learned to take time to laugh, as it is truly the best medicine. I learned to set time for friends, and not to blame others for my internal feelings. I found that doing inexpensive activities with friends and family, like cooking, hiking, dancing, swimming, or seeing free live music, helped me feel more bonded and built up my endorphins. And if you are feeling down about yourself, social media isn't the best for healing, since comparing your life to others' only brings forth mixed emotions about the trajectory of your life.

Happiness comes from the inside, not solely from another person, nor from a job. The right people will love you for who you are, not for the job you do or for the amount of money you make. They will support you even when the rest of your life isn't going well. It is important to remember to have a positive sense of self so that it translates to future relationships, both personal and professional.

Chapter 15

Get This Headset Off Of Me!

One job always available, even during a recession, is work as a telemarketer. I had not been able to keep a job for more than 11 months since graduating from college. Too many precarious situations kept coming up to put me out. After being let go from a failing company and collecting unemployment checks for about three months, I finally found a job that seemed stable. It was by no means a dream job, but it was with an established company, and the work environment seemed to be a step up from the other sketchy jobs I had before. I was thrilled to be getting a guaranteed base salary, commissions, a youthful working environment, health benefits, and a potential 401k!

I was hired to work for a company we will call Media Looks, a digital sales and advertising company. Media Looks partners with a couple thousand associations and sells advertising space for them either directly on their website, via e-mail campaigns or through directory guides. For instance, the American Society of Interior Designers has professional members (individuals; interior designers) and company/business members (essentially exhibitors at trade shows; supply companies). All of the members can go to the association's website or subscribe to their newsletter to be up to date on industry information. We would call to convince the company members, or other related companies who sold relevant products or services (i.e. furniture, paint, custom windows), to buy banner ads or newsletter spots to be seen by all of the individual professionals in the field of interior design. The goal would be that the interior designers would click the ads and read more about the product or service offered by the advertised company.

Media Looks is a melting pot for young college graduates in the Dallas area. Everyone knows everyone, who knows someone else. It's like the game "Six Degrees of Kevin Bacon."[xxii] When I interviewed for the job, they showed me the wall of "All-Stars" from which I recognized a few people on it from my high school! Getting a job there is enticing because of the promise of making big commissions, a young company culture, and hell, there is a beer fridge on almost every floor!

The interview process for the job was fairly extensive. I had to pass a phone screening, then a few casual interviews, and then I was invited back for an eight-person panel interview. Coming from an outside sales job, I was used to meeting and interviewing with people at a moment's notice. I aced

---

[xxii] Six Degrees of Kevin Bacon is a game based on the "six degrees of separation" concept, which assumes that any two people on Earth are six or fewer acquaintance links apart.

all the interviews, and they called and hired me that same day. I started work a couple of weeks later.

There were 16 of us hired at the same time, and we were split into two training classes. One was a class of fresh-out-of-college 22-year-olds, and the other class was composed of those of us who were in our later twenties and had a bit of work experience. I was the only lady in my training class other than the young woman who was our trainer.

Of the 600 or so people in the company, around 400—including myself—were in media sales. Media sales happened to be a glorified call center. Our job was to wear headsets all day long and make hundreds of calls trying to pitch and sell ad space to companies. Some of the skills we picked up from this job were valuable, yet it was mentally exhausting. The days when I was making sale after sale were exhilarating. *ChaChing!* Other days were mind-scrambling.

Everyone was separated into small teams of about eight. Our team leaders were people who had been promoted after proving themselves to be positive and consistent at making sales. Usually these people were young—sometimes younger than me. They were forced by management to be strict with us. We had "minute minimums" that were difficult to reach some days. We were expected to have 140 minutes of talk time each day. Now, to someone who has not worked in a call center, that may not sound like much. But factor in all the calls that go unanswered, calls where you are hung up on, and calls that go straight to voicemail, plus the time you try to write e-mails, sort leads, and look at company websites—there was little to no downtime. We had two required 15 minute breaks every few hours to help us recharge, but those 15 minutes seemed to disappear faster than a bottle of champagne on New Year's Eve.

Since I had already put in countless hours of cold calling at my previous job at the daily deal company, I wore down fast. A lot of people did. Several co-workers just decided to walk out or not come back because they could not imagine being forced to make another phone call. This job took a certain type of personality and an ability to push through high stress. You always had to be "on." Having a rough day? *Too bad*! You must constantly be making contact with other human beings. In fact, out of my initial training class of eight, only three of us made it past the first couple of months.

My second month on the training floor of about 80 people, I was ranked number two in sales, outdone only by my team lead. I came to realize that good sales often correlated with having the right project, meaning selling a product for a well-recognized association. My team had lucked out and had the right project at the right time. That, combined with diligent work on my part, meant I saw sales rolling in. I was determined to keep up the pace.

One afternoon during a break, I checked the flashing light on my cell phone. I had received a message that a friend's husband had died in the line of duty in Afghanistan. I felt the ripple effect of chills going up and down my body. My own challenges seemed tiny next to the realization that someone I knew had died after being attacked trying to protect our country. I excused myself to the bathroom, where I sat for ten minutes allowing the tears to fall down my face. Unsure of why I felt this burst of emotion over someone I barely knew, I collected myself and my thoughts, and went back to my desk. My emotions stemmed from the grave news, but also from the remembrance of all the young men and women who sacrifice so much every day for America. Later, after I'd been making cold calls for an hour, I made the largest sale on the floor that day. I went home declaring that this small victory for me was in honor of those who work so much harder. It was a reminder that the world is so much bigger than our day-to-day lives.

Shortly after that incident, I was promoted to another team off the training floor, making me the first of my group to move up and out of training. And then work life changed. I wasn't a newbie anymore. There were higher expectations, and more team meetings were required to "help" perfect our sales pitches. It seemed to me like time was spent ridiculing us for lackluster sales or bad pitches. They took time away from our phone time to get on us about not having enough talk time, but still expected us to meet the required talk time!

The purpose of this company was sales, sales, sales. It didn't matter if what you were selling was not an effective product. It didn't matter if you avoided mentioning certain facts about the product to potential clients. The VP of Media Looks would send out angry mass e-mails to the company if talk time was low or if we had not met our monetary goal. Sometimes, he would hold us past closing time because there had to be a certain dollar amount on the dashboard. It was our job to keep the company thriving.

Despite being at the top of my team several times, there were points when I wanted to scream: *Get this headset off of me!* I would go home from work and head straight to bed. Some days I just wanted to curl into a ball and not worry about the stress of making a sale every day; the stress of making enough commission to pay my bills. I would have nightmares about the damn headset literally being stuck to my head and that I couldn't ever take it off. I dreamed I had to wear it on first dates, out at parties, and even in the shower! I would watch TV and read books to forget about my own day. But I could not get my mind off those damn headsets. I would grow jealous that the characters in TV shows were not forced to wear headsets all day long. I longed for a time when I would not have to be on the phone for what seemed like every second of every day.

It wasn't just the headsets at this job that bothered me. Big Brother was always watching. The company had a "digital dashboard" where we could see how many sales and the number of minutes every single person had in real-time. Every call we made was monitored and audio recorded for legal purposes. This made sense for purposes of going back to track a call or retrieve lost information. But Media Looks had a team of people that would listen in and judge our phone calls based on our sales pitches. The company had a strict sales pitch intro and certain talking points you had to hit on each call. The pitch did make sense, and it worked to many people's benefit. We learned that we didn't want to waste a pitch on an administrative assistant. The goal was to get straight to the decision maker. We spent tedious hours practicing, coming into work early and having separate meetings to go over what worked and what didn't. We would sometimes be given grades for our pitches. Some people's pitches got picked apart in meetings in front of everyone! Luckily, none of my sales calls were ever chosen for public scrutiny. I cringed for the people who were judged in front of the whole team just to prove the point that some of us were not so good at following the pitch—and therefore that must be the reason sales were lacking. The managers measured each project with the same rubric. They blamed all lack of sales on the quality of the pitch or on lack of minutes on the phone. But this simply didn't reflect the true situation. Some people on upper levels that had better projects to pitch were making only a few phone calls a day and raking in sales of over $50,000 a month. Those of us on the lower levels had to compensate for the shitty projects we had to pitch (projects that had a track record of being difficult to sell or were a bad product overall) by being required to be on the phone for hours of talk time. You had to survive a lot of stress and bullshit to keep moving up, and potentially make some awesome money. *That which is life...*

If the sales reps do well, the company grows, and so to pass on the success, the top sellers were often given special treatment, like first access to the beer fridge on Fridays, cash prizes, paid trips, or better projects! But many people did not do well with the high stress and endless phone calls. The company hired new people every few weeks because the turnover was so high. A desk buddy would be there one day and gone the next.

Personally, I was miserable. It became a struggle for me to make it to work by 7:00 or 7:30 in the morning every day. Some of the people who were fresh out of college found instant connections and friends to help them get by. I, on the other hand, had a hard time making real connections with anyone at Media Looks. Sure, I got along with people, but since I was not happy at the job, I wasn't putting myself out there. The team leads was oblivious to my inner struggles. One thanked me for my positive attitude and my ability to come in every day with a smile. He said I was good motivation for others on the team. Even though I was being described this way, on the inside, I was trying to form an escape plan, like a cat quietly waiting for the right moment to bolt out the door to freedom. My bones ached to quit, but how tedious it had been to find a decent paying job.

During my time at Media Looks, several people got fired for "looping." Looping is when you call a number you know has a long voice mail or a long automated system with choices of where to direct the call, and you essentially loop through the system, pressing numbers, just to get talk time. It's a crazy world when people feel so pressured to meet performance standards that they feel forced to break the rules. I was only four months in when I started looping.

I was always behind on my minutes. I'm a fast talker, so most of my sales were made on phone calls that took less than five to ten minutes. I didn't shillyshally around on the calls; I got straight to the point. And even if I had made the highest sales of the day, it didn't matter. If I wasn't on the phone talking someone's ear off to meet my minutes, I would have to stay late. I spent more time worrying about what my minutes looked like on the dashboard than actually taking in the fact that my sales were good. I started to call numbers I knew would have a long intro or hold time. I would call the weather channel for an update. I would call a joke network for the daily joke. *What did the cat say when he lost all his money? I'm paw!*

I knew that someday, Big Brother would stumble upon these "illicit" calls, but I was willing to take the risk just so I could keep up with minute minimums. The policy didn't make sense to me. I felt like people should concentrate on what is important (actual sales), not the amount of time it took to make a sale. Coming from a job where all my sales meetings were outside the office and not monitored, it felt like I was back in high school with all the rules and regulations. A month went by with my occasional looping, and no one had noticed.

It was finally time for Christmas break. By some miracle, we were given two weeks off! I felt lucky and grateful, but the drawback was that pay would not include commission during this time. Let me tell you, it was two of the best weeks of freedom I had ever had. I felt like a normal member of society, as I was able to come and go as I pleased without feeling overwhelmed by the pressure in and on my head (*those damn headsets!*). I dreaded returning, but when those two weeks were over, I dragged my tail back into the office. On my first three days back, I made a sale every day. In fact, I had just wrapped up making a sale when I was called into the head floor manager's office. I noticed that my team lead was missing too. I saw the foreshadowing.

At Media Looks, all work space is set up in an open floor plan. The desks are right next to each other. The music is loud, and the people are louder. Yet somehow, when you are on the phone, you are expected to zone everything out and concentrate on the person on the other end. Even the people who have offices do not have privacy, as the doors and walls are glass. I went into one of those glass offices that day, where the head floor manager and my team lead were already waiting for me. For a long time, every time I got called into a boss's office my stomach knotted up. I had been laid off or put in so many awkward work situations in bosses' offices that it seemed natural to assume I was in trouble. *They knew.*

Big Brother had listened to a few of my calls and had found some of my bogus dials. They tried to play back a few calls to show me the proof, but I cut them off. I admitted to looping occasionally. I said I understood that they had a "zero tolerance" policy. I wasn't the first and I wouldn't be the last. I thanked them for everything I had learned and for the fact that they had taken a chance on me. They told me they wished it didn't have to be this way, but I had made a poor decision and they couldn't keep me on board. I handed over my badge and proceeded to head back to my desk.

While packing up my notepads and pictures, my pod asked me if I had been promoted to another level. In a casual tone I told them, "Nah, I just got fired." No one believed me. They thought I was joking. I admitted to what I had done. They were all shocked, paranoid, and angry, because they were in disbelief that I would be the person to be looping, since I seemed so positive and did pretty well in sales.

Just as I was done packing up my desk, I saw that all the team leads had just been released from a meeting. I could tell by their judging looks that it had been about me. About how I had made a mistake. About how they needed to monitor their teams to catch these instances. Everyone was glancing my way, giving me disappointed or angry looks. *Did they really have no understanding of why so many people ended up trying to fake talk time?*

I held my head high. I walked out of the building that afternoon not knowing what my future held, but still, I felt a sense of relief. Like all the pressure of the world had been released from my body. But as quickly as I felt that relief, the heaviness came rushing back. I had only been at that corporate job for five months. It was barely 2013, and I was already starting out the year unemployed. As suddenly as I had scurried out of unemployment, here I was again, but this time with no benefits package or health insurance. I usually try to take the high road, but sometimes in life you choose the low road that doesn't lead you in the right direction. Unbeknownst to me, I was wandering into my longest stint of unemployment to date.

I had been through direct sales, outside sales, inside sales—the works! I knew that I was done trying to make sales work for me. As much as I did not like many of my sales jobs or the situations I went through, I can't help but be appreciative for the life lessons the jobs taught me.

I learned perseverance, determination and self-reliance. I learned to be confident in myself and to step out of my comfort zone. I learned that if you don't ask, the answer will always be *no*. I learned to deal with rejection. I learned to push myself mentally. I learned to listen—and I mean really listen—to what people have to say. I learned how to find interests in common with strangers. I learned how to be "to the point", because time is valuable. I learned how to negotiate. I learned how to ask a lot of questions, and to not be afraid to ask the difficult or scary ones. I learned sales tactics to use in life, as well as the ones to watch out for.

I learned what I did and didn't like about certain jobs. I learned what makes an honest and ethical person. I learned from others' mistakes, but most importantly, I learned from my own. I learned that everything I had experienced so far was to help me become a better person, employee and decision maker.

Chapter 16

Currently Seeking: Perfection

During my times of unemployment I regularly posted my resume online on job sites like Indeed, in the hopes of catching someone's attention. I was called and e-mailed several times every week by recruiters. They would enthusiastically ask me questions and then say they thought I was a good fit for the job opening they had, which was usually a sales job. Many would have me drive to their staffing firms for a sit-down interview.

I learned that this was standard practice; recruiting firms vet you before they even present your information to the hiring client. The problem was, when a recruiter thought I was a fit for a job, it was because I had so much sales experience on my resume. But deep down, I knew that a sales job was not what I was looking for. I was tired of the high stress levels that working in sales entailed. I seldom got calls about jobs I might have preferred.[xxiii]

[xxiii] I did however, catch a break later down the line, and ended up getting my highest paying job ever through a corporate recruiter!

I have been on at least eight interviews with recruiters for outsourced jobs, and four interviews to become a recruiter myself, one of which led to a job offer. But after learning more about what recruiters actually do, I declined the offer. The interviews I went on to become a recruiter were extensive, usually hitting the two-hour mark. Being people persons, the recruiters with whom I interviewed were happy to answer all the professional queries I had about the business. I also know a handful of people who graduated from college and went on to be recruiters, so I asked them what the job was actually like. I learned the ins and outs and what exactly the job requires. From all the information I gathered, I am able to tell you some secrets about the staffing industry I wish I had known when trying to trek my way through the job jungle.

What I learned is that recruiting isn't a normal sales job. Recruiters are not selling a product. They are selling people. Above-average recruiters need to know their product (people) and what the market demands. And the market is always changing. Supply and demand are what make a candidate hot or not. Recruiters judge you on the first meeting. If they do not like something you say or wear, they may not even risk presenting you to a client. They have to be picky, because they have to meet the needs of their clients. Recruiters know from a quick scan of your resume whether or not you have potential to a client. Perhaps your education and skill set are great, but not needed at the time. Many recruiters will simply hang on to strong resumes until a suitable job match comes up.

It's also a numbers game. They are trying to meet a quota for number of calls, number of in-office interviews, and number of job placements. If they fail to place candidates and bill clients, they do not meet quotas and risk losing their own jobs. It's somewhat of an oxymoron: find people jobs, or you can't keep yours!

Recruiters are hired by companies to make placements for hard-to-fill jobs or jobs that require a very special person with a very particular set of skills. They are looking for their Liam Neeson.[xxiv] Most recruiters are not meant to find job placements for the young and recently graduated, although many recruiters themselves are just that. It may seem that they care about helping you find a job, but often, they are just looking out for themselves. Who can blame them? With such high pressure and even higher turnover rates, it takes a special kind of person to be able to do the job correctly. There may be recruiters out there who genuinely care about finding people work, but the environment they work in is so heavily based on numbers and commissions that the pressure can get to their heads. New recruiters are often excited about being able to help people find jobs, but they will be pushed by upper management to hit certain "sales" goals, which can be rough. An inexperienced recruiter will likely only work for the numbers, instead of truly working with job seekers to find them leads and potential careers. It can grow increasingly frustrating for the recruiter, too, trying to find the "perfect" person—who may not even exist—for a hard-to-fill position.

I also learned that jobs posted online for months that are never filled may not even be real. Some recruiting firms may post phony jobs to collect as many resumes as possible for jobs that are in high supply. A firm is only

---

[xxiv] In reference to the 2009 movie *Taken*.

as good as their inventory. The more people they have in their inventory, the more likely they are to make a placement—and a commission check. The practice of posting phony jobs online is unethical and unsettling, but according to my recruiter friends, it does happen. Whether we like it or not, this practice highlights the fact that resumes are the first marketing opportunity we have for ourselves. If you are doubtful about the quality of your resume, your best bet would be to ask a recruiter what skills and jobs are hot, so you can tailor your resume to stand out!

If you do not hear back from a recruiter you are often left wondering why. You spend a good 30 minutes on the phone with them and another hour in the office, and another 30 minutes to an hour filling out paperwork or taking a job placement test. You could do this over and over again and still not hear back from anyone. It is probably because the recruiter just did not see you as a good fit and moved on. In business, hearing nothing usually means "not interested!" Many times, a recruiter will present your resume to a hiring company's HR department, and then the recruiter never hears back from the company. This brings the entire process to a standstill and the recruiter will avoid you so they do not have to explain what is going on.

The general consensus from those I know in the staffing industry is that your best bet when working with a recruiter is to work with a firm that specializes in finding the type of job you want. Randomly contacting a recruiter with your unsolicited resume and asking them to find you a job is not a good tactic. Answering a recruiter's job posting with your resume and a message that says you think you are a match for a position they are looking to fill *is* a good idea. Calling to follow up doesn't hurt. The name of the game is matching your skills and experience to a specific job the recruiter is already working on. That's why most recruiters don't return calls or e-mails from candidates that don't match all the requirements of their current job searches. For them, time is money, and they only make money on matches!

I believe that in the long run, in order for jobs to be filled in a timelier manner, employers should invest in training employees. Instead of waiting for the impossibly perfect person, companies should take some time to educate and mold new hires into the "perfect fit." According to an article in *Time Magazine* in 2012, employers are often unwilling to provide extra training or education to their employees.[66] A 2013 Accenture survey found that only 21 percent of U.S. employees had received any formal employer-provided training in the past five years.

According to my research, some business owners are hesitant to invest in training their employees because they cannot afford the investment, or they are worried that training employees will make them better equipped to leave for some other company. But if schools are not preparing people for the workforce, then companies must step in to teach necessary skills to people with potential. Otherwise, jobs will stay unnecessarily unfilled, and the work will not get done. Employers need to hire the best people they can find, and prepare them through the right kind of focused training and development programs. Investing in developing employee capital can increase job productivity and potentially profits for the company as well.

What you don't learn from recruiters or school is how to interpret the jargon you see in job postings. Here is the insider's edition of the real meaning behind those common phrases. *(Caution: Satire proceeds!)*

ENTRY-LEVEL POSITION
You will be making just over minimum wage doing menial tasks. But it's a resume builder!

ENTRY-LEVEL POSITION IN AN UP-AND-COMING COMPANY
You will be making just over minimum wage doing menial tasks for a company that has no idea what it is doing, and may go under in a year.

COMPETITIVE SALARY
You will be paid slightly less than the industry average. You may find yourself working your ass off for that 32 cents an hour raise at the end of the year!

JOIN OUR FAST-PACED COMPANY
Everyone is running around like a cat chasing its own tail. You will not receive formal training, but they will expect you to catch up quickly.

IMMEDIATE OPENING
They are desperate for desperate people.

SALES POSITION REQUIRING MOTIVATED SELF-STARTER
You will have to supply your own car, phone, laptop and leads. It's like owning your own business without getting to be your own boss.

SELF-MOTIVATED
Must have the ability to put up with bullshit on a daily basis and still act gung-ho about the opportunity to work there.

WE OFFER GREAT BENEFITS
You get health insurance, but only the bare minimum, and half of the costs will be deducted from your paycheck. Oh, but they offer free peanuts in the break room! Sometimes even cookies!

PENSION/RETIREMENT BENEFITS
After six years with the company, you will finally be 100 percent vested!!

SEEKING ENTHUSIASTIC, FUN, HARD-WORKING PEOPLE
You must have more of a personality than some of the drones they have working for them. But you will be expected to work like said machine.

CASUAL WORK ATMOSPHERE
You can wear jeans to work, maybe get away with having a tattoo, but will have to tolerate your co-workers making poop jokes or calling you a lame nickname like Snassulfruss.

COMPETITIVE ENVIRONMENT
You will be working with people who think they are running a national league football team. No one lasts longer than six months. Sometimes people cry.

JOIN OUR DYNAMIC TEAM
This job will keep you guessing. Your job description will likely change a lot. Or your boss will be bi-polar and may take you for sushi one day and throw a stapler at you the next.

FUN WORK ENVIRONMENT
They have nerf guns at the office that you will often find being shot into your coffee or the back of your head. They have "team bonding" happy hours that consist of everyone trash talking their bosses.

A DRUG-FREE WORK ENVIRONMENT
You will be drug tested. But employees just fake the drug tests anyway. Or they take legal prescription anti-depressants or drink a lot of alcohol to soothe the workday pains.

MUST BE DEADLINE ORIENTED
You will be expected to work beyond the traditional 8-5. On your first day, you will already be behind schedule.

SALARY RANGE $xK-$xK
You will probably be told the higher end of the spectrum, and then actually be offered the lower end. But again, they offer free peanuts in the breakroom!

A HIGHLY VISIBLE POSITION
You will likely be client facing and have to put on a fake smile a lot. Or you will be working in an open floor plan environment where everyone can see your random Google habits.

FLEXIBLE HOURS
They will change your schedule up on you to fit their needs, not yours. When you request time off, the system in place to do so will not be so easy or flexible.

DUTIES WILL VARY
People will try to get you to do their job for them.

WHERE EMPLOYEES FEEL VALUED
You get access to the best parking spot if the other employees vote for you as Employee of the Month! Free lunch is offered... once a month.

MUST HAVE AN EYE FOR DETAIL
No one else will cover your ass when you make a mistake.

COLLEGE DEGREE PREFERRED
College degree REQUIRED! But only the "useful" ones.

CAREER-MINDED
You will be expected to be responsive at all times. Meaning, you better have e-mail on your phone and check it even when you're on vacation skiing down the mountain.

SEEKING CANDIDATES WITH A WIDE VARIETY OF EXPERIENCE
You'll need it to replace three people who just left. You may be required to do the jobs of those three people for a fraction of the cost. Meaning they will need you to be able to use Photoshop, Salesforce, QuickBooks and take the trash out for the night.

PROBLEM-SOLVING SKILLS A MUST

You are walking into a company with a bunch of people who like to gossip and cause drama. Office pranksters might also be a problem. The background of your computer may often be changed to weird images, like a GIF of a dancing topless Grandpa.

REQUIRES TEAM LEADERSHIP SKILLS

You will need to act like a manager, but not get the pay rate of one.

GOOD COMMUNICATION SKILLS

Because no one else at the company will be able to relay information correctly.

ABILITY TO HANDLE A HEAVY WORKLOAD

You must have the ability to work 60 hours and get paid for 40... and not complain.

ASPIRATIONS FOR GROWTH WITHIN OUR COMPANY

If you're a suck up, you might have a chance at that coat closet for an office instead of a gray cube!

Chapter 17

Health Care Conditions

After I graduated from college in 2009, like many other college graduates, I had no health insurance. At that time, once young adults were no longer students or hit age 19, we could no longer be covered by our parents' insurance. I found myself without insurance many times during my first few years out of college. I had a few jobs that did not even offer insurance while I was working. Like many young Americans, I simply could not afford to enroll in a private plan. I knew it wasn't ideal to go without health insurance, because even if you are a generally healthy person, there are still important reasons to go to the doctor every year. It's not like you can just do a WebMD search every time you feel sick. You may just determine you are either pregnant or dying every time! Or misreading information and going around arguing nonsense beliefs.

Self-diagnosed 1: "I'm anti-biotic!"

Self-diagnosed 2: "No way, man, I'm pro-biotic!"

Changes:

In March, 2010, Congress implemented the Affordable Care Act, or, as some call it, ObamaCare—since the legislation was proposed by President Obama. At the time, I was not even sure what the new law was; my only opinion was that I was thankful for a part of it. My sister and I were both uninsured at the time, and we both were able to get back on our dad's insurance until we turned 26, because the new law enabled adult children to stay on our parents' insurance until we hit that magic age. This was a blessing for us and many of my friends. After this change, I began to wonder, what exactly is the state of healthcare in America? How has insurance and laws changed in recent years? How does it all affect young people, women, and those with lower incomes?

The Affordable Care Act made changes that affected everybody. Preventive care rose to the top as a vital issue, and it became part of all health care plans. One of the biggest changes included Medicaid expansion to more than just a select group, and it filled in some of the existing gaps of the public program to provide extra coverage and access to health benefits for more people. Historically, Medicaid only covered low-income children, pregnant women, elderly and disabled individuals, and some parents, but excluded other low-income adults. Medicaid's expansion was done to make health care more readily available.[67] But Medicaid expansion is up to the states, and some have found themselves stuck up a tree where they cannot get the affordable insurance they want and need.

According to Obamacarefacts.com, before the Affordable Care Act law, health insurance policies had "lifetime caps." Simply put, if your cap was $2,000,000, you would no longer have insurance the moment your insurer spent every last dollar of that limit. Younger adults who came down with a sudden serious illness or were victims of an accident could easily reach that limit. Infants with serious diseases such as a birth-induced illness requiring surgery and special care units with prolonged hospital stays could run out of health insurance before reaching the age of two. But ObamaCare eliminated all those caps, which alleviated a huge source of anxiety for people who face the future with chronic health problems.

One in two young people technically has a pre-existing condition, which could have been grounds for being denied coverage before the Affordable Care Act became law. One in six young adults has a chronic illness like cancer, diabetes or asthma. I have friends in their twenties with Crohn's disease, lupus, and multiple sclerosis. I know a lot of people who have some sort of health issue they must deal with on an ongoing basis, and it made me wonder about the costs these people must pay just to live a normal life—and our lives are now longer than ever. In the 1930's we could make it to 60. Now we live, on average, about 80 years!

In the past, insurance companies were charging women higher premiums than men for the same plans. The U.S. Department of Health and Human Services highlights the fact that previously, a 22-year-old woman could have been charged a premium 150 percent higher than a 22-year-old man only because she's a woman.[68] As a result of the ACA, this became illegal.

The ACA was also designed to improve the health of all pregnant women and newborns, and to allow women to determine the course of our own lives. The ACA actually expanded the availability of women's preventative care, such as pap smears, screenings and counseling. It also made birth control and emergency contraception more readily available for women. Maternity care became one of the "essential benefits" that was added on all new individual and small group policies. An expectant parent obtains coverage in every state during open enrollment or during a special enrollment period triggered by a qualifying event. But this special insurance enrollment period begins only after a birth. As a result, uninsured women who learn they are pregnant outside of the regular three-month open enrollment period, can get stuck paying thousands of dollars for prenatal care and delivery—or worse, going without care. Unfortunately, with some plans, being covered by insurance also does not guarantee that child birth costs will be low.

For those women not ready for parenthood, the added "contraceptive mandate" proved helpful. This meant that companies offering their employees' health insurance would have to provide plans that covered all approved contraception methods at no extra cost to their employees, such as birth control pills, Plan B, and intrauterine devices. Because of this mandate, by mid-2015, reports show that women saved $1.4 billion since the law went into effect.[69]

Oppositions:

These advancements for women have been fiercely challenged. The contraceptive mandate did not sit well with many people or companies with religious backgrounds. Arts-and-crafts chain Hobby Lobby, along with a few other businesses, took the government to court on the grounds that their views were protected by the Religious Freedom Restoration Act (RFRA). The Supreme Court ruled in their favor, saying that certain "closely held" for-profit businesses can cite religious objections to opt out of the requirement to provide free contraceptive coverage for their employees. The 5-4 decision in favor of Hobby Lobby marks the first time the court has ruled that for-profit businesses can cite religious views under federal law.

People on the Internet and the media boomed with outrage. Many were upset that for-profit businesses had been deemed "people," and that their beliefs standing against actual people (women) were outrageous. This was stepping on the separation of church and state issue. They argued that an employer shouldn't have control over what medications women take. People across the country raised their voices to say that these businesses have no idea what it is like to be a low-income woman who has trouble paying for emergency contraception.

Others looked at the ruling as a triumph for religious freedom, and stood by the fact that government cannot make laws to burden those beliefs. Some argued that birth control is not a constitutional right, and that it is the responsibility of the woman who wants/ needs these services, and that it is not up to the company to pay to cover such a personal decision. Others claimed the case wasn't about religion at all, but just a way for conservative companies to make a stand against ObamaCare and the impact of certain laws on American people and corporations.

The Hobby Lobby case actually brought up bigger questions: Who should be paying for our health insurance? What should be covered? Is health care a right or a privilege? These issues affect all Americans, but one of the groups being impacted the most, is young people. According to Obamacarefacts.com, a whopping 43 percent of uninsured people are young adults between the ages of 18 and 35 (about 17.8 million).

Arguments over the ACA and replacement plans continue to cause a storm of heated debate. People against the ACA claim it is "unconstitutional" for health insurance to be mandatory, or for the "individual mandate" to exist, which is a penalty tax required of those who do not enroll in health insurance. There are hardship exceptions to these rules, but the law made no exemption based only on employment status; it's all about yearly income. People rightfully became upset that insurance companies canceled many of their plans because their old policies didn't cover the ACA's 10 "essential benefits" which includes services that not everyone uses, like mental health care or maternity care. For those who lost their private insurance, the replacement plans cost more than the plans offered before.

Oh, baby:

Right before the changes brought about by ObamaCare, my sister became pregnant—at 20 years young. Let's just say, the sperm donor was not in the picture. It was a trying time, as my family struggled to figure out our options. Hayley, who had worked as a waitress most of her adult life, was not offered company insurance. Our family was not quite sure how we would finance my sister's and the baby's health. Dallas is also one of the most expensive cities to give birth in the U.S.[70]

Prior to 2014 when many revisions to health care laws were made, women who purchased health insurance were often out of luck if we wanted to have coverage for maternity care. In 2013, the National Women's Law Center reported that just twelve percent of individual market plans included maternity benefits. Pregnancy itself was also considered a pre-existing condition that would prevent an expectant parent from obtaining coverage in all but five states. This meant that if you were not extremely low income, most of the bills that come from having a baby were your own responsibility.

Every hospital also has their own costs for prenatal care, delivery, drugs and prescriptions, and care after birth. If you do have insurance, you must pay your full deductible for both the baby, and yourself, and then see bills pile up if your insurance does not cover a decent percentage of the costs associated with maternity care. Delivery costs vary widely across the United States, and even within individual cities. There is no set fixed rate, meaning many may be sticker shocked by the final bill. From 2004 to 2010, the prices that insurers paid for childbirth rose 49 percent for vaginal births and 41 percent for Caesarean sections in the United States, with average out-of-pocket costs rising fourfold, according to a report by Truven.[71] The average total price charged for pregnancy and newborn care was about $30,000 for a vaginal delivery and $50,000 for a C-section, with commercial insurers paying out an average of $18,329 and $27,866.

The ACA put a cap on out of pocket costs when insured in network, but it has varied every year, close to $7,000 for individuals and upward of $13,000 for families.[72] That does not include the monthly costs paid out of pocket to have health insurance.

After extensive interviews, paperwork, and review, because of my sister's low income, she received Medicaid to ensure the baby was born healthy. According to the government website, Medicaid plays a key role in child and maternal health, financing 40 percent of all births in the United States. Medicaid coverage for pregnant women includes prenatal care through the pregnancy, labor, and delivery, and care for 60 days postpartum, as well as other pregnancy-related care. Medicaid is controlled by the state and helps cover other health-related costs for people who simply cannot afford it. This is literally a life-saver in many situations.

Another option for my sister's care would have been Planned Parenthood, a chain of clinics that provides low-income women with the medical attention all women need.[xxv] But living in Dallas, Planned Parenthood was not the best option since it was the center of intense debate in the state's ongoing battle around abortion, which is only a small percentage of the services they offer. The state ended up closing down most of its locations due to politics.

I still can't comprehend all the feelings that were brought forth the day I found out about my sister's pregnancy. Questions about my sister's future stared us down. What would be best for her and the baby? When in a situation like this, family and friends can weigh in with his or her thoughts, but the ultimate decisions are up to the expecting mother. After we all weighed the pros and cons of each option, Hayley decided it would be best to find adoptive parents for the baby.

Through an agency, she received scrapbook after scrapbook from couples that were eager to adopt a newborn. The thoughtful pages were filled with pictures of happy couples, their pets and homes, as well as descriptions of their jobs, beliefs, and personal lives. Given the options available, in a case like this, you just have to go with your heart. You

---

[xxv] I swear, if it were not for Planned Parenthood, more women would resort to using fish antibiotics or shooting apple cider vinegar up their lady parts just to cure a UTI! Yes, this is a real thing.

have to decide the fate of a child based on raw intuition. That is just what Hayley did. She chose a middle-aged couple in Austin, Texas who could not have babies of their own, and had an adoption fall through in the past. Their background story and current activities and jobs resonated with my sister. The fact that many of their friends also adopted children meant her baby would grow up in an understanding environment.

My sister gave birth to a little girl. The adoption was the right decision at the time for my sister because she was nowhere near being financially stable or mature enough to take care of a little life. Holding that baby for the first time was one of the most honest and pure moments in my life. Hayley was so heroic in her journey, and I admire her for making sure her baby grew up in a happy home. Every year, we receive pictures of her growth; her cute little dimples and perfect strawberry hair. One day, when she becomes curious about her biological family, we will be ready to share stories. We are thankful that my sister was able to get the Medicaid she needed to have a healthy baby.

This is why the expansion of Medicaid and women's health coverage on insurance plans is so important moving forward. If my sister's income had been slightly more, Medicaid would not have qualified her as "categorically needy." Instead, she would have spend more time proving herself as "medically needy." Private health insurance would have considered her pregnancy a pre-existing condition, and therefore little to no coverage would be offered. Also, the lack of control of the prices for childbirth leave many worrying about the debt associated with being able to bring a newborn safely into this world. Women should have the flexibility to choose birthing options, and not be burdened by the ever-increasing costs of labor and care, or restricted access to birth control and family planning for political reasons.

Health care shopping:

In response to the issues around the much-needed health care reform, the government developed a website to help provide people with health insurance, which launched in December, 2013. Healthcare.gov, built by 55 contractors, is one of the most complex pieces of software ever created for the federal government, utilizing real time communications and interactions with at least 112 different computer systems across the country. In the first ten days it received 14.6 million unique visits, according to the Obama administration. The purpose of Healthcare.gov was to be a one-stop shop for people to see if they qualify for Medicaid, subsidies, exemptions and discounted private insurance plans based on income, age, current wellness, and location. Sure, you could go right to a private provider, but the purpose of the site was to be sure Americans knew their options.

There were heated discussions all over the media about how the new system was full of glitches, and how the website itself was downright awful and crashed from server overload. It was actually kind of funny what a big deal people made about the fact that the site was not perfect right off the bat. *Many Americans waited decades for easy access to health care, but if a website takes too long to load they give up and click over to YouTube to laugh at cats falling off of furniture.* It's like the site needed its own doctor to bring it back to life! But in reality, the government launched it before it was ready. They should have waited. *It wasn't as if we had not had deadlines pushed back before…*

The reported problem with the site was that it could not handle the number of people accessing it. People would register, and then the system would not acknowledge that they had ever set foot on the site. The system would tell some people they did not qualify for Medicaid, even if they did, or vice versa. Pages within the site seemed to be missing. Customer support was not much help. Reports sent to insurance companies were said to be duplicated, or too confusing for insurance companies to know who their new customers were. Penalties for failure to enroll in health care kept getting pushed out. The site took several more months to get up to speed.

On a positive note, a statement from President Obama in the spring of 2015 indicated that the Affordable Care Act had helped cover 20 million people, six million of which are adults under 26. According to the "National Health Interview Survey," the share of young adults 25 and under without health insurance coverage is the lowest young adult uninsured rate recorded since they began using its current design in 1997.[73] Analysts predict that coverage will continue to expand in the years ahead, as long as the law and one-stop shop websites, or something similar remains in effect.

Under the Affordable Care Act, basically five levels of available health insurance plans were issued: Platinum, Gold, Silver, Bronze, and what I like to call the "Cat Plan," or what insurers call the Catastrophic plan. Catastrophic health insurance plans are primarily reserved for people younger than 30. The "Cat Plan" is designed to cover you if you break a leg, get in a car accident, or are diagnosed with a major illness, because it's not like we cats actually have nine lives. The Affordable Care Act's Catastrophic plans (which are different from similar plans offered before) added three annual primary care visits and preventive services at no extra cost, including disease screenings and vaccinations—a definite improvement for young people who need these plans. But it is important to remember that under these plans, insurance companies will not pay any bill outside of what they deem preventative care, until you have paid the full deductible, which varies by plan, but usually amounts to several thousands of dollars. So if you need a cat scan, watch out for the price!

Accidents:

On September 26, 2012 I turned 26. It came faster than I ever could have imagined. My golden birthday offered me no "Gold Plan." I had not been at my job long enough to "earn" insurance, and I could not be on my dad's plan any longer, so for that short period of time, I was without insurance… again! It was expensive to buy insurance for just three months, which was the time it would take for me to wait out the enrollment period. I joked that I would make sure to wrap myself in pillows if going for a bike ride, and brew my own herbal tea filled with apple cider vinegar, bear berries, root of ginger, and eye of newt, sure to wane off all germs. *It's a miracle nothing major happened to me.*

That same year, my 25-year-old unemployed then-boyfriend, Wyatt, made a stupid decision and leaped into a moving car, causing him to dislocate his shoulder. Everyone has a dumb accident story, right? His arm looked like it was being held on by a thread. He wasn't sure if he had insurance, and his excruciating pain was amplified by the fact that he was worried this little visit to the ER would cost him thousands of dollars. Luckily, after being pumped full of pain relief drugs, he found out he was covered. He had been re-added to his mom's insurance just *days* before the mishap. He got lucky.

What if an accident affects your ability to make money to pay your bills? A friend's 24-year-old brother went on a lake trip, and jumped into what he didn't know was shallow water, landed precariously, and damaged his spine. He had to be airlifted to a hospital where surgeons spent more than five hours working on him. He endured vertebrae damage, affecting his ability to walk, work, and take care of himself as he once did. His friends raised $59,000 on GoFundMe for his surgeries, rehabilitation, and for cash to get by. Of note is the high number of pages on group funding sites with outcries for help about health related issues. This is indicative of how much America is in need of better access to affordable health care.

There are countless examples. Accidents are never planned, and some people spend their whole lives trying to pay for events that happen to them unexpectedly. Injury-related visits to emergency rooms are far more common among young adults than among either children or older adults. According to the Commonwealth Fund, in 2010, the prevalence of injury-related visits to the emergency room was 1,187 per 10,000 among 18-to-24-year-old females and 1,547 per 10,000 among 18-to-24-year-old males —which is the highest rate of all the age groups.[74] Average emergency room costs vary widely based on treatment, but a 2013 National Institute of Health study put the median cost at $1,233.[75]

Costs:

CNN said that 60 percent of all bankruptcies are due to medical bills, many of which are unexpected and unaccounted for.[76] A study by the Commonwealth Fund found that emergency situations and unavoidable health care situations have caused 72 percent of people to be burdened with serious medical debt while unemployed. Also, 72 percent of people who lost their health insurance when they lost their jobs skipped getting needed treatments or preventive care, or filling prescriptions due to cost concerns. Being un(der)employed risks people's health, since so many people rely on their employers to help out with insurance.

When you make very little money, even a visit to the doctor or the price of a common drug is too high when you have other bills piling up. It's not uncommon for young people with little income who cannot afford to pay hundreds of dollars a month for insurance to say, *"I literally can't afford to be sick. I can't get the antibiotics I need to cure this infection. I can't get a physician to get my blood drawn to make sure everything is okay. I cannot address the stomach pains I have been enduring lately. I can't get new glasses to help me read or drive."*

The biggest problem for low-income young adults is the lack of Medicaid expansion in every state. Only about half of all states decided to expand their Medicaid programs under the ACA to add coverage for young individuals, young families, and those at the federal poverty level. Young adults with low and moderate incomes continue to suffer from the highest rates of being uninsured.[77]

The burden of medical bills and debt has significant financial consequences for young adults, forcing many to make education and career trade-offs. According to the Commonwealth Fund, in 2012, among young adults who reported problems paying medical bills or said they were paying off medical debt, 43 percent said they had used up all their savings to pay their bills, 33 percent had taken on credit card debt, and 32 percent had been unable to meet other debt obligations such as school loans or tuition payments. 31 percent delayed education or career plans, and 28 percent said they had been unable to pay for basic necessities like food or rent.[78]

Affordability, rather than a belief that they do not need insurance, has been the major barrier to young adults gaining insurance coverage in the United States. The previously stated Commonwealth Fund survey provides considerable evidence that most young adults enroll in health insurance plans when they have access to affordable coverage. Nearly two-thirds of young working adults of ages 19 to 29 who were eligible for coverage through their jobs enrolled in their employers' health plans. The survey asked those young adults who did not take up employers' offers of coverage why they had not enrolled. Only six percent said they did not need coverage. Most said their reasons were either because they had insurance under a parent's plan, had coverage through a spouse or partner, or said the coverage was just too expensive.

A big problem with the Affordable Care Act is that it didn't actually do anything to control costs associated with health care; it mainly made insurance easier to find and available to more people. Maybe it should be just called the "Available Care Act." It may be easier for many to view health care options, but the costs are not necessarily affordable for everyone. The hidden fact is that the ACA needs young people to sign up to help premiums stay low for everyone. Young adults are a crucial component of the Affordable Care Act. When enrolled in coverage, they provide premium revenue to insurers and generally have small payouts for claims. To keep plans viable and affordable for everyone, insurers need healthy, relatively low-cost young adults to enroll.

Under the ACA, people with household incomes up to 133 percent of the federal poverty level (about $14,400 for individuals, or $29,300 for a family of four) received Medicaid regardless of whether they meet any of the other conditions of need.[79] The loosened eligibility requirements caused an enormous increase of millions of Americans to switch from private insurance to public insurance, which increased public's costs. ObamaCare's Medicaid expansion was paid for through a combination of tax increases and cuts to Medicare (which affects people like the elderly and disabled). Monthly rates and deductibles are reported to be high for those who are not deemed "poor."

Plus, Medicaid only covers doctors within the network, which has become more limited, which means people do not have the freedom to choose whatever doctor they would like. A 2012 Physicians Foundation survey, of more than 13,500 doctors from around the country, found that 26 percent cut services for Medicaid patients due to costs[80] Government-run programs and insurance can also cap earnings for doctors, which cause some specialists to simply not accept any insurance, and set their own cash-only a la carte prices for their services. This already happened to a small degree under the ACA. That same survey found nearly seven percent of doctors planned to switch to cash-only practices.

One of the biggest problems is that the U.S. continues to treat health care as if it is a commodity to be purchased, rather than a social service to be provided. The U.S. is the only rich country that does not offer a publicly funded health system, relying instead largely on private insurance.

The consequences of this can be seen in the fact that health care costs in this country are far above those of any other advanced country. Unlike countries where universal health coverage is in place, the negotiating is left to individual care providers, rather than using a publicly funded buyer that can negotiate a fair price for the drug. Higher drug prices result in higher premiums.[81]

The United Kingdom's National Health Service, for example, purchases drugs for the entire country's supply, known as a formulary. But in the United States, we have individual insurance groups and hospitals that buy for their individual consumers, resulting in an unregulated variety of pricing.[82] According to the International Federation of Health Plans, Americans pay anywhere from two to six times more than the rest of the world for brand name prescription drugs. Medicaid cannot, by law, negotiate with pharmaceuticals, which to some may seem crazy! Other countries, such as France, Germany, Spain, and Japan, regulate fees, charges, and insurance premiums to ensure that the system is affordable for the society, while still maintaining universal access to health care. But on the flipside, this does delay access to new drugs, whereas the United States has access to innovative and lifesaving drugs almost immediately.

Like all businesses, private insurance runs as a business and exists to make money. The cost of bringing a drug into the U.S. market is higher, partially because of marketing expenses. The United States is one of only two countries (New Zealand being the other) that allows direct-to-consumer advertisement of prescription drugs, while elsewhere promotion is limited to medical professionals.[83] Strict regulations are placed on these ads, but this does raise the cost of the drug so Big Pharma can see a return on investment.

Another issue is that the cost of services and procedures are often hidden from the consumer. Many people do not ask about the prices for surgery or prescriptions and get stuck with a high bill they didn't know was coming. What's worse is that you might end up not knowing the cost of a medical bill until you see the number itself on the final bill. Price and outcome transparency in the health care industry needs to be implemented. In the U.S., everyone should know about the Healthcare Blue Book, which is like the Kelley Blue Book for cars. It offers fair pricing for medical procedures so that people can find the best option. It's also important to not be afraid to ask your doctor or pharmacist for more details on costs to avoid fees you can't afford.

If all that cost talk makes your head spin, we can just refer to the "Adorable Care Act": a Tumblr owned by Organizing for Action, filled with cute kittens, baby seals and panda cubs encouraging us all to get health insurance. *Aww!*

Sick and family leave:

Sick leave is not properly engrained in our society. When we do not have insurance or paid time off, the ability to take a break when sick, or to take care of a family member or a new born baby is difficult. President

Obama pointed out in a State of the Union address that the U.S. is the only advanced economy that doesn't mandate paid sick or maternity leave for its workers. Of the developed countries, the United States is in a bracket with the smallest percentage of people receiving the benefit in practice, with an estimated 10 to 32 percent of the population eligible for paid leave. No other developed country is below 33 percent.[84]

In January 2015, President Barack Obama asked Congress to pass the Healthy Families Act under which employees could earn one hour of paid time for every 30 hours they work, up to seven days, or 56 hours of paid sick leave annually. If passed it would apply to employers with 15 or more employees, for staff as defined in the Fair Labor Standards Act. Paid sick leave advocates state that providing paid sick time can reduce turnover, increase productivity and reduce the spread of contamination in the workplace.

The U.S. does guarantee *unpaid* leave for serious illnesses through the Family and Medical Leave Act (FMLA). But low-wage workers are often excluded from unpaid family leave. While the Act guarantees all workers up to twelve weeks of unpaid leave to care for a new child or sick family member, it applies only to businesses with more than 50 employees, only covers workers that have been with an employer for at least one year, and doesn't extend to part-time workers. These exemptions are significant; it makes it so that just over half of American workers and less than a fifth of all new mothers are actually covered by FMLA.[85] And this largely affects women since we are more likely than men to take time off, reduce work hours, opt for positions with more flexible schedules, or quit work altogether to care for a child or another family member.[86] This is also a major contributor to the overall gender pay gap.

Of course, lack of leave isn't the only factor making it difficult for average workers to juggle child-rearing and a job. The lack of subsidized child care is another. One of my college roommates and her husband had twins in their late twenties. But there were many complications in the delivery of the girls and also in my friend's health. The babies were unable to be sent home from the hospital for two months, racking up medical fees and undeniable stress on the new parents.

One child is hard enough to prepare for, but two at once made my friends take a hard look at budgets and child care options. Would child care for two even be worth going back to a job because all of her pay would practically go toward the expenses of day care? In this instance, she took a year off to strictly stay home with the babies, and then later enrolled them in day care.

Some people do not have a choice. The need for money takes valuable time away from people to care for their own body or the body of a loved one, like a sick child or parent. Those who could technically take more time off may feel pressured by the 24/7 workplace culture and return sooner than later.

Cats march:

The 2016 election of Donald Trump as the next American president spread uncertainty among those who stand strong with the progress in health care and women's rights. Trump's voice and actions toward women before and during his campaign had shocking effects. In the media he spoke of his opinions that women should be judged based on looks, women should not be paid more than the husband because it spells "trouble," women who choose to get abortions should be punished, that sexual assault in the military should be expected, that he's pro the defunding of Planned Parenthood, and that his first order of business would be to repeal and replace the ACA.

Trump's negative remarks rang powerfully not just in America, but all over the world. On January 21, 2017, women gathered to march in the "Women's March on Washington." The march drew at least half a million in Washington, and some estimates put worldwide participation at 4.8 million, according to Womensmarch.com. At least 408 marches were planned in the U.S. and 168 in 81 other countries.[87] It is considered the largest one-day march in American history, and was streamed live so even more could view as if we were there.[88]

The Women's March was organized as a grassroots movement and aimed to send a bold message to the Trump administration. Women and men alike marched in masses to show their passion for the protection of women's rights and other causes including health care reform, women's equality and workers' rights. Many were concerned that in 2017, the United States' rank dropped to 45th in the World Economic Forum's Global Gender Gap Report.[89] The availability of parental leave, childcare assistance, and access to affordable women's health care affect the United States' rankings.

Pink knitted hats with little cat ears could be seen on thousands as they stood for their causes. The people were now literally dressed like cats to make a unique statement. *The cats be marching! Hear them roar!* The Pussyhat Project was a nationwide effort initiated by Krista Suh and Jayna Zweiman of Los Angeles which resulted in masses of pink kitties standing out across the aerial views of the events. Many of the hats worn by marchers were created by crafters who were unable to attend personally, and wished them to be worn by those who could.

A long way to go:

Health care reform, as we all know, is a complex and complicated beast. Many concerns and questions remain unanswered. The United States has some of the best doctors and health care in the world, but these things come with a price.

People debate whether the federal government should stay out of the health care business altogether, leave it up to the states, or on the opposite end, start a single payer program and just get out of private insurance. The argument is that a public single payer system (i.e. Medicare for all) could save money by reducing administrative costs and help regulate and set standard prices for services across the board, but still offer the delivery of care by private businesses. Many argue that the U.S. should look to other countries that have better health care access and affordability. But no country's health care system is perfect.

The implementation of the ACA and expansion of Medicaid was a way to quickly get more people covered, but Medicaid has been plagued by concerns about its quality, access, and financing virtually since its inception. It is feared that without more reform of our health care system, costs will continue to rise and be a burden upon those who are hardworking tax payers.

As one of the first acts of his presidency, Trump's administration wrote a whole new health care bill, but when the time came to vote in March of 2017, The GOP actually pulled it from the house floor due to its rushed nature, lack of support because of speculation that the plan would end up covering less people, that it would allow insurers to sell lower-quality insurance, and raise prices for the poor.

Lobbying also happens all around us, in which different companies and organizations spend millions of dollars to have people figure out which bills will have the biggest effect—positive or negative—on their business and where voters stand on those bills. Lobbying exists to help sway policymakers toward a decision in a person's or company's favor. Lobbyists speak with committees, coalition groups, legislators and their aids, to voice their position on a bill's language. The Center for Responsive Politics reports that the health care industry spent more than $500 million in 2015 and again in 2016 lobbying on health care issues, which is more than any other sector.[90] And that's just the money which is actually reported! It's tough to produce any big changes when a multi-million dollar industry is constantly playing a game of tug of war. As hard as you fight for something you believe in, there is always someone fighting just as hard on the opposing end.

The changes caused by the ACA were designed to try to provide people with the care we need to get through life. Life is full of unexpected events, so shouldn't we have better access to health care and modern medicine? A great mass of Americans still do not have health care. The best way to reform health care is yet to be determined, and new bills will continue to be written for the foreseeable future, but at least the ACA provided change and more awareness to larger issues. The United States would do well to make health care more about accessibility and sensible prices, no matter age, income or wellness!

Chapter 18

Shafū

"In the middle of a world that had always been a bit mad, the cat walks with confidence."

Rosanne Amberson

After six long and grueling months of unemployment following my stint at Media Looks, which drained my savings, no American company came to my rescue. Instead, I was offered jobs at both a British company and a Japanese company. I had the opportunity to be surrounded by people with different accents, and due to many factors (never mind that I can't take English accents seriously; they either make me giggle or make me mad), I decided that my best bet would be to work for the Japanese manufacturer. This cat was making a transition from unemployed to a place I thought would have a good *shafū* (company culture)!

The company's U.S. focus is pet products. My job description included copywriting and editing marketing and sales content, providing sales support and reports, planning and executing annual trade shows, and working on promotions, social media, online and print marketing and advertising, budgets, press releases, customer relations and new business development. I was excited to finally have a "big girl" job!

This was a situation where I found my own life reflecting what studies show: that unemployment delays gains in experience, which can lead to a loss in wages. This company quoted my starting pay over the phone, but then a day later they found out I had made less at my last job (they were not taking commission into account), and that I had been fired, so they came back and told me that they were going to pay me $2,000 less a year than they originally offered. It wasn't fair, but since I hadn't signed paperwork on the quote they'd given me over the phone, I still accepted the offer. Six months of unemployment had taken its toll. I was ready to work!

The U.S. office only consisted of nine staff members. I was the youngest, and only one of two Americans. Our small office was culturally diverse. We didn't just have Japanese and American staff. At any given time there were up to five languages being spoken. Growing up in California and Texas, which are melting pots of cultures, I embraced the diversity.

After only three weeks on the job, the company sent me to Las Vegas where I experienced my first industry trade show. Many companies in the pet industry go to these types of shows to present their products to buyers who include everyone from major name stores to boutiques. I had fun meeting and greeting, and felt I was off to a great start. I got to attend the annual poodle competition at the Mandalay Bay Convention Center where I saw dogs spray-painted to look like bright orange tigers, purple zebras, Muppets, or rainbows. Every size poodle, from toy to giant, was represented, trimmed to perfection with their round tails held high. I was in heaven seeing dogs of all sorts, from Chihuahuas in strollers, to baby Corgis that looked like teddy bears, to Mastiffs clomping through the aisles.

There was no official training at this job. I was just thrown in there and had to pick up the pieces from the last person in my position. After a few months' time I started to find my footing and began to form changes that made a difference. *This was the stepping-stone I needed to get out of my funk!* I had my own office and a flexible lunch break, as well as the ability to present new ideas, travel, and learn more about marketing and manufacturing. The way the company had run marketing in the past was sub-par, and I came up with a revamped agenda. Not only did I raise traffic to the company website, I also took it upon myself to find ways in the budget to save and reallocate money to be focused more on online adverting. The company sells all of their products through e-commerce, yet did not spend valuable time and money to implement online marketing strategies, such as Google AdWords campaigns or outreach to pet bloggers and dog trainers. They had ignored the upkeep of their own website and their content management system.

I was under the impression that the job was indeed salaried, but that turned out not to be the case. A couple of months after I was hired, the company introduced a time clock computer system, where we were told to clock in and out every day, because apparently we were being paid hourly. No big deal, I thought. It was a more trustworthy way to keep track of time instead of estimating on paper time sheets. It was all gravy, until the clock on the server became six minutes ahead. If I showed up right at 9:00, because the server's clock was off, I showed as clocking in at 9:06. I never thought anything of it, because I assumed management knew the clock was wrong.

It took them a year to mention anything to me about all the "late times." Management decided to count me late for several days instead of admitting that the clock was, indeed, wrong, and this affected my performance review. It affected my co-workers as well. Even after several of us explained our case, management said we were supposed to adjust ourselves to the clock, instead of them adjusting the clock to be correct. Mysteriously, the clock was fixed after that round of performance reviews.

But several months later, the clock jumped ahead a few minutes again. I didn't want to be lectured again for something so dumb, so when our outsourced IT guy came to update the server, I simply asked him to set the clock back on the server to the correct time. It took him all of four seconds, which was much shorter than the time it took for administration to go through all the "late" times, print it all out, present the times to the Japanese supervisors, lecture those who were "late" several times, and then use that as the reason for us not to receive a raise. If they cared that much, why did it take them so long to mention it? Many of us were frustrated, because we felt we should be held accountable for adhering to real time, not made-up time. But this was just one small hint of the issues to come.

In America, for the most part, we stress working in deadline-driven environments. But some cultures tend to take their time. At this Japanese company, corporate decision-making goes though many stages along the corporate hierarchy. Their decisions were very cautious and conservative, and were made more slowly than I was used to. This was no fast-paced environment. There was a lot of sitting around waiting for projects to get approved. We would have meeting after meeting, even if we covered the same topic over and over again. And to get any task passed, four signatures were required.

The Japanese are known for making work a priority in life. Frequent travel and long hours can take a toll on anyone. Ironically, it was not uncommon for our Japanese president or manager to appear to be napping during meetings when they came to town. I would go on and on about analytics or marketing plans to people who were sleeping! In Japanese culture, sleeping at work is so common that there is actually a word for it: *Inemuri*. It roughly translates to "present while asleep." In Japan, people get respect for giving their best which could mean pushing themselves to exhaustion. Therefore, showing how tired you are is a statement; it says you're a hard worker. In this context, it's easy to understand why people get away with sleeping at work. Co-workers assume the sleeping person must be working too hard. But apparently there are rules to sleeping on the job. You must sit up and look engaged (despite the fact that you're asleep). It must appear that you could wake up at any moment and have a great idea! *Oh, don't mind me. I was just taking a cat nap in my office because I have been diligently waiting for months for a project to be approved.*

(^._.^)/

In our office, the Director of Operations, who was also the sole HR person, was known for her micro-managing ways. She often would come up with new rules that didn't make sense. But instead of talking directly to people about the new rules, she would usually have the Director of Sales and Marketing relay the message. He didn't agree to all the rules, but she was the office head honcho (when the Japanese leaders were home in Japan) so he had to go along with what she decided.

By this time in my life I had witnessed questionable or counterproductive policies implemented by higher-ups on a regular basis. Every company has its own rules, many of which have no effect on the productivity of the company. Often, corporate policies prevent companies from functioning effectively. The "rules" implemented by the Director of Operations reminded me of Professor Umbridge from *Harry Potter*, and her constant declaration of restrictions, except on a more toned down scale. I was told not to sit at my desk with my knee up, as it was "unprofessional." *Never mind that I was in my own office all day . . . alone.* I was told not to have books on my desk because "we don't want people to get the wrong idea."

What . . . that I like to expand my horizons? Could I not read on my lunch break? I was advised not to get personal mail delivered to the office, even though everyone received industry mail and small packages all the time. The reason I was given was that she "just didn't like it." Out of nowhere, a new dress code was enforced, banning jeans. *You know, because we had no client interaction and sat alone all day... that made sense.* We were even told to take a particular route through the office to get to the restroom!

In the middle of our office was a showroom of all the pet products, for easy access. The showroom was a workspace designed for those of us in customer service and marketing to be able to see the products up close so we could answer customer questions via e-mail or phone. Having the products in the showroom made it easier to see exact measurements, how the products work, or describe the parts included. It was also an area we used to prep for trade shows. But the Director did not like us going in there, and she threatened to put a lock on the showroom door. It was like she wanted to keep it as a shrine of products. The fact that she wanted to make it more difficult for us to access made no sense, since the space should have existed to help us do our jobs better.

Sometimes she would state rules, and then only enforce them on certain people, or never bring them up again. The list of silly rules went on and on, and it seemed there were new ones popping up all the time, none of which were regularly enforced or consistent. I just learned to roll with the punches, because in the long run, these rules were minuscule, compared to the grand scheme of life.

But there was one new rule applied to everyone that sent me over the edge. The Director of Operations announced that if we did not work exactly 40 hours per week, we would be punished by having four hours of vacation time taken away from our allocated days—even if we missed the 40 hours by just five minutes. We also had to work exactly eight hours every day and could not, say, allocate more hours to one day and less to another, but still end up with a total of 40 hours. Somehow the numbers had to be perfect!

What I witnessed as a result of this draconian rule was employees' lack of initiative to stay late since we were unable to split our 40 hours up. Now, if we stayed late to take a call from Japan, we would be forced into overtime, which also had to be approved. Luckily, we were paid time and a half for overtime. But the company was no more productive than before. The new policy just made the employees resentful. Instead of motivating us to be more productive by sharing company goals or giving projects or team exercises to help company morale[xxvi] and productivity, the new policy just made us watch the clock in fear of not meeting the "perfect" number of hours.

Why the need for such control and punishment in such a small office? Shouldn't managers be more worried about the actual work that goes into making a company successful, instead of micro-managing their employees? Not every job can be measured by an arbitrarily imposed numerical standard. It also was upsetting to me because I often did not have 40 hours' worth of work to do. I would ask for more work, but many

---

[xxvi] Anytime I say "morale", I say it more like "meworwl" because that is a distinct sound my cat Oliver likes to make in the morning when trying to get me out of bed. Stop staring at me, cat!

times my requests were ignored. If they wanted to pay me for 40 hours' worth of work, that was fine, but sitting there for hours, feeling bound by the hands of time with little to do is enough to make a girl go crazy! I get it, when you get paid to do work, companies have the right to set the rules. But how can they expect to retain good people if they create an unsavory work environment?

The employees at the company felt trapped, because we couldn't go to HR—because there was no official HR. When there is no one to trust or talk to about workplace practices that feel unfair, it creates a negative thought spiral for employees. There should always be someone to go to with questions and concerns, but we just did not have that. So we often complained amongst ourselves, which just made us angrier.

The issues ran deeper. Upper management from Japan was constantly making business decisions that made no sense to the other employees. Inventory mistakes were being made left and right by higher ups. The two U.S. office managers were engaged in a long-term, childish feud. Communication was poor, meetings never started on time, deadlines were missed, cash flow was questionable, and budgets were never set.

After two years, it started to feel like I was stuck in a rut. There was no room for advancement (people who had been there for five to ten years were still in the same positions), no raises to look forward to, and no experienced mentors to help me learn and grow. My e-mails and reports suddenly went ignored, admittedly so, by office managers who said they simply "did not have time"—even though those reports were insightful. It felt like no one acknowledged my hard work or how I had helped grow the brand name. I was expected to put in so many hours, but many felt wasted. Of course I was grateful for many aspects of the job, but the company environment was not one I felt was best for my growth. If you don't feel challenged or appreciated, or don't agree with the *shafū*, that is when you know it's time to start looking for new opportunities and make like a cat and scat.

I started putting my whiskers out there by letting friends, old colleagues, and recruiters know that I was looking for new opportunities. As luck would have it, I found a new job through a company recruiter who reached out to me on LinkedIn about furthering my career. The new company was also willing to offer me a 35 percent pay increase and travel opportunities!

The same week I put in my two weeks' notice to leave for my new job was the same week my marketing/sales manager was let go. It left an uneasy feeling inside of me, because he was often the one sticking up for the other employees and would agree that the many rules set in place were unnecessary. But it also made me feel that leaving was the right decision. It was time for this *neko*[xxvii] to wave her goodbyes.

More than one-in-three American workers today are Millennials and have surpassed Generation X as the largest share of the American

---

[xxvii] Means "cat" in Japanese.

workforce.[91] We will have more of a say in what we want in the marketplace, workplace and what will keep us at a job. As tough as it is to find a job, we all know it is just as hard to find one worth staying at. Gallup estimates that Millennial turnover costs the U.S. economy $30.5 billion annually. As Generation Y looks to find our new work homes, companies are going to have to create working environments that will keep our fresh minds on board.

What Millennials are looking for in a job varies, but many can agree that what helps us stay is company culture. Does the company have a mission statement the team can relate to? Does the company embrace new technologies or provide training? Do they recognize hard work or achievements? Do they plan work events or team building exercises? Does the company have flexible hours? Are they transparent with all their employees? Does the company do anything to make a difference in the world?

What I have observed throughout my many jobs is that companies often enforce policies that can pressure employees into breaking rules. What every manager needs to learn, however, is a principle well established in the social sciences: the more rules you throw in people's way, the more we want to subvert them, because that's the only way we can resist being infantilized. Good managers focus on changing the rules and regulations that do not work, and do not make a big deal about rules that have no effect on the sales or the performance of the company. Results are more important than enforcing ridiculous rules.

I have worked at companies that did not have their employees' best interests, or the company's—or both—in mind. This is why there is so much failure amongst companies where management is unwilling to make positive changes in the workplace or form decisions that evolve with the times. Teams of innovative people should be working toward a common goal. If no goals are in place or if there is no open conversation, how can one expect a company or an individual to flourish?

Opportunity for growth is a factor that is important to Gen Y. If we do not feel like there is any room to make a difference or move up, you can bet that we will pounce at a chance to go somewhere else where we will feel more valued. 76 percent of Millennials think professional development opportunities are one of the most important elements of company culture.[92] Feeling valued and working for a boss who is motivational are top reasons people stay at a job. If we have neither, then what is the point? Where some people are learning to settle, others are learning not to. We all define success differently, but a big part of feeling successful is being engaged and thriving. If we do not see ourselves making a difference in a good way, we may not stay, no matter how high the pay. Fighting through "dumbemployment" is a waste of time.

Many young people want flexibility when it comes to personal time. We do not like to feel threatened by management or feel like we are members of an assembly line. We want to be able to travel, attend to personal matters, and to have time to go to the doctor for preventive health visits. We do not want to feel like life is just work and that our personal lives always come second. We want to know that if we need a break, it's okay to take five and watch a cat video. Just tell your boss that a study done at Hiroshima University in Japan proved that looking at cute animals improves workers' productivity and ability to tackle difficult or long tasks because it heightens moods.[93] *Now all those inspirational cat posters in workplaces make sense!*

Types of bosses are varied: the ones who care, the ones who don't, the ones who get paid absurdly more than anyone else, the ones who seem like they don't know anything, or think they know everything, the ones who pick favorites, the ones who micro-manage... and, if we are lucky, the ones who are actually good at their job, open to innovative ideas, and are good mentors. Workers want managers who offer feedback and helpful hints. We look for people who inspire us to work hard and contribute to a company's success. We all want a positive environment. But in many of the dead-end jobs that young adults work, we are missing valuable mentors to help us learn and grow.

There are no perfect employees, and there are no perfect employers. The best we can do is to try to work together to produce the best cohesive work environment that suits both parties. As Millennials come into our full maturity, we become empowered by what we learn from our experiences to help change workplace culture for the better.

Chapter 19

Coming Of Age With Social Media And Rapid Technology

In a way that previous generations cannot fathom, Gen Y has seen a rapid evolution—a revolution, really—in society due to technology. Technology is moving full speed ahead in the fields of medicine, personal appliances and communications. As Millennials, we have seen the progression of technology over our lifetimes—and oh, how quickly everything has changed! The older half of the Millennial spectrum have an understanding of the old world as well as the new age. Machines are so integrated into our lives now that our kids (existent or nonexistent for now) will find it difficult to believe the stories we will tell of how it used to be when we were growing up. Technology has moved so fast that even some younger Millennials have completely different recollections of tech, and do not remember much of life without advanced technology. A lot can happen over the course of one generation.

Older Millennials remember life *without* cell phones and the Internet. We remember having to do research papers in the library using a good old-fashioned encyclopedia set, taking notes on notecards, and later we were introduced to web searches *before* Google took over. We can remember typewriters, fax machines, our first desktop computers, the age of dial-up Internet, AIM, and our first e-mail address. We can remember using our parents' records, floppy discs, cassette tapes, and VHSs, and then progressing to shiny DVDs, CDs, and the on to downloading invisible (sometimes illegal) MP3s. We remember pagers, the first Nokia "brick" cell phone, our first text messages to our best friend, our first camera phone, and watching our first hilarious cat video on YouTube. We remember the first iPhone and the models that followed which caused endless lines outside of stores, and the first time we heard someone say, "There's an app for that!" We remember the progression of desktops to laptops to tablets to everything being saved in "clouds." We remember the rise of blogs, or submitting our first Tweet. We can remember when we joined Myspace or Facebook and all the social media sites that followed. Facebook was even invented by a member of our generation, and it changed how we view ourselves and other people. "Liking" something or someone can now be confused for another meaning.

Social media makes it easy for us to immerse ourselves in worlds that we would not have seen so readily available in the past. Any information is just a click away. We can view and communicate with friends, strangers, and even celebrities from all across the world. We can see the effects it has on bringing people together who have a common goal, mindset or want to start a movement. We can now learn more about how people live and think all over the world, especially when it comes to current events. No longer are social injustices such as police brutalities or acts of racism just swept under the rug, because people film and share these instances in real time with smart phones, making it difficult to ignore outcries.

But social media *(the real Y2K bug!)* has also led to a viral outbreak of people creating an online image of the person we want to be and want to seem to be to others.[xxviii] It also provides more of an opportunity for us to compare ourselves to others. Everyone does it; it's inevitable. We can judge whether we feel on track, ahead, or behind our peers, financially and emotionally. If we haven't reached a certain point by a certain time, we wonder, *where is my dream job? When will I feel like a grown up? When will I be on a path to financial freedom?* We can easily experience feelings of jealousy, depression, and hostility when viewing life in this open medium. Some will seem to have it all figured out. Some will seem like they are still experimenting. Some will be proud and outlandish, while others will just be social viewers. Few will shy away and not get involved online, and will seem to have disappeared. Seeing people every day on social media that you know get married, get promoted, buy houses, have babies, get advanced degrees and travel through Europe can be overwhelming when those milestones are not happening in your own life. No longer are ten-year high school reunions as much of a surprise, because people can keep updated through an updated visual yearbook and a multitude of social apps to see how each other's lives are moving

---

[xxviii] Did a catfish get ya?

along—although, seeing people in person and talking directly face-to-face can change one person's view of another in just a short conversation. Never in the past has a generation had to endure so much of their existence and coming of age in a world where everything is out in the open, and also open to interpretation. But what we see online is rarely the true and whole story. It is unfair to compare one's whole life to just a page of someone else's.

We can also use comparisons to realize just how unique and different we are. The struggles, achievements, and life events we each individually live, shape who we are to become, and help motivate us to become the adults we want to be. "Coming of age" has various meanings to different people and to different generations. It should be our goals and achievement and life standards that uphold our feelings of self-worth, rather than how many "likes" or "re-tweets" we get. Now traditional rites of passage ceremonies are not exactly true testaments of our growth. Just because two people are the same age does not mean they have reached adulthood at the same time. We might feel we are not an adult until we reach a certain milestone, such as living alone, getting married, obtaining a certain income, or overcoming a tough life event that makes us feel worthy of calling our self a "man" or a "woman."

Technology and social media have affected the entire job market and the way people find and keep jobs. These two items have made some jobs obsolete, but invented new ones too. These have changed the transparency of business. Websites like Glassdoor.com make it easy for people to find companies and read current employee perspectives, likes and dislikes about the company and their jobs, interview tips and salary ranges within the company. Social media has made us more of an open book to prospective employers as well.

We now use e-mail, cell phones and the Internet to keep us in the loop. Some jobs expect you to always be "on" and ready to respond. No longer are work hours so defined by specific hours or location. Various computer programs help us do our job more easily and complete tasks quickly. It causes us question how on earth people could have done a similar job just 30 years ago, without the convenience of so many advances in the technological landscape.

It can be argued that technology could have made our lives easier and given us the ability to work less hours and allowed more time for our interests. Instead, many of us find ourselves working much more, or trying to use technology to fill the void of wasted time when we are expected or forced to be at "work." Technology has increased productivity, but it has also hindered it. It has caused workaholics to work more and slackers to slack more.

This generation is used to having things obtainable at our fingertips at all times because of advances in technology. Smartphones and credit cards make our lives easier. They increase efficiency and convenience, but can also lead to debt, lack of self-control, and impatience. It's harder than ever to wait for anything we want because we are used to having it available in seconds, with or without cash flow. But having things more easily obtainable does not establish financial stability. We are now labeled "aspiring adults" who have most of the knowledge and maturity to make it, but don't necessarily make enough money, or have the right job yet. It takes time to develop the skills needed to run a successful business or grow in a career. It takes education, dedication, patience, and consistency.

In a world where the current generations are accustomed to having everything at the tip of our fingers to access instantly, are we now growing increasingly frustrated because success does not happen instantaneously? We should be aware that we will run into some jammed doors along the way of finding success. But smart cats are persistent enough to keep on pawing until that door finally cracks a bit and then swings open.

We look to older generations and see all the wealth and abundance they have built, and, for a brief moment, we get lost in the thought that we should be able to just enjoy what has been developed. But with time and age, many of us realize that we cannot just revel in the accomplishments and expect more to just come our way. There will always be great advances, but there will also be obstacles in our way no matter how old we grow, what decade we were born, or what part of society we live in. We have to remember what other generations went through to make our world what it is. It is through much struggle that we have the equal rights we have. Older generations have made civil rights a reality, allowed us all to be able to vote, and helped us make gay marriage legal. We are learning from our elders' successes and mistakes and trying to develop new ways of thinking about the environment and healthier lifestyles, and lending energy to a growing acceptance for people from diverse backgrounds.

What the majority of Millennials believe in is based on history, as well as the present. We are shaped by the economy, technology, other people, and the events of our times, such as the 9/11 terrorist attacks, going through two wars and seeing peers give their lives for our country, seeing the crisis of mass gun shootings, cities destroyed due to climate change, and of course, the effects of the Great Recession.

We may have inherited a lot of problems, but we have also inherited a lot of opportunities. If an older generation can go all the way to the moon and back, how far can we Millennials go with our understandings, social connections and new technologies? The world continues to evolve and change, and so should the structure of society. If we don't learn from history and past mistakes and try to build a better future, what good will this particular generation do for our country and the world?

Finding our self-worth and where we belong in this world is fundamental in developing ourselves on the inside so we can change the outside world. What we Millennials have achieved in this world so far is based on our ability to innovate and observe, and the courage to be different. We have the right to pursue what we want to do and become who we need to be. The inventors of Facebook, Spotify, Groupon, and Nasty Gal are all Millennials, and they have been motivators for others to take their backgrounds, educations and instincts and try to do something new.

We cannot let ourselves be defeated by the hardships placed before us. We cannot just have a blasé attitude toward the future. We cannot just shrug our shoulders and say, *"Whelp... the cats be unemployed..."* every time we hear a news story about lackluster job growth, or slashes to school and health care budgets. We cannot be passive progressive. In times like these, we should let our thoughts be known by using the technology that is so readily available to us. We can vote (local is where some big changes start), we can create petitions, we can write to our representatives, we can do our research and become educated. We can enlighten others, invest our time and money in programs we believe in, we can brainstorm, build movements, hit the streets, and demand change. What generation hasn't had to work harder than before to create the change they wish to see?

As we come of age in the modern world, we need to have an entrepreneur's outlook, a healthy sense of self, the ability to learn from others, and a working knowledge of the world and its new and ever-changing technologies. These will be the keys to help us find gainful employment, financial freedom, and continue to make changes in society.

Chapter 20

Quarter Life Crisis

"*Adulthood always felt like something we were sneaking into together.*

Can't everyone see that, as far as these things go, I am a series of cats standing on one another's shoulder inside a big coat? If you could just sit in your apartment all day being a bunch of cats, it would not be so bad. But you have to go outside and pass among people. And you never feel that you are doing a very convincing job. You get back indoors and peel off the coat, gasping with relief. 'Whew,' you say. 'Fooled them again.'"

Alexandra Petri
A Field Guide to Awkward Silences
Penguin, 2015

My whole life, I've had dreams of losing my teeth. Dreams where I would be sitting in class and my teeth would grow the length of a saber-toothed cat and then fall out. Dreams where my teeth would crumble into little pieces and I would constantly have to spit them out. I always wake up in a panic because the dreams feel so real. It turns out dreams like this are very common amongst people who are unsure of the future. Dreaming about teeth falling out represents feelings of insecurity and inadequacy, and such dreams often occur at a transitional period in a person's life. This is because losing teeth is associated with the loss of childhood innocence. The dreams could also be revealing anxieties of getting older. This made sense. Especially during times of unemployment, I had constant dreams relating to the distress I experienced trying to grow up and be a functional part of society.

When I was a teen and naive, I assumed that by my mid-twenties, I would have life all figured out. I assumed I would have graduated from college, be living on my own or maybe married, working a job I liked, making good money, and living in the city, where I would be happy. I would be surrounded by friends and family, clinking glasses at dinner parties talking about how our lives had all come together.

Fast forward to my mid-twenties. I was still struggling to decide what to be and how to get there. I saw people who seemed to be ahead of the game, like my friends who were already married and owned a house by 25. But many others were still laboring their way through school or working in a dead end job. The common theme of a "quarter life crisis" became a trend among peers in their twenties and early thirties. Of course, no one was where we had imagined we would be, according to the societal standards we'd grown up with. We now claim "adulting" is hard. *Please don't make me adult today. Today I want to cat!*

One day during my 24th year of life, I was having one of those weeks. Like the old saying goes, "When it rains, it pours." All in the same week, I had quit a no-good scam of a job, my laptop got a virus and crashed, and it was time to say goodbye to my (now ex) fiancé at the airport so he could go back to grad school. After dropping him off for what I didn't know would be the last time, I headed home, contemplating where my life was going. *When would my boyfriend and I be able to live in the same city? How would I pay to fix my computer to apply for jobs? How could I become more independent? What is it I want to do with my life?*

As I headed toward the tollbooths at the airport exit, I suddenly realized my brakes were not responding. This is my worst fear when it comes to driving; having no control of the trajectory or speed of the car! Just as I was questioning my life's trajectory, my car would not stop going forward. In a panic, I kept pumping the brakes, and the car slowed down slightly, but not enough to potentially keep me from hitting anyone who got too close. I just happened to be at a location in the airport that had a shoulder lane. In a state of fear, I veered to the side. I pulled the emergency brake up and then frantically pulled the key out of the ignition, even though the car was not in park *(Oops!)*. My car shook like an earthquake, and for a moment, I thought it might explode! I stopped on the shoulder just inches before hitting a sign that read: "No Parking."

After bursting into crocodile tears, I called my dad and was able to convey that, by some miracle, I was okay. I didn't hurt anyone or anything. I had caught a break when I couldn't even use my brakes. As I sat stone cold in my car, I kept mulling over the fact that I now had no job, no place of my own, no computer and now, no car. It seemed there was no end to my misfortunes.

I realized that sometimes you just don't feel like you have control over your own life. Sometimes you feel like it's either moving too fast or too slow, and it's hard to tell what speed or direction it's going to take. The truth is, we don't really know where life is going to take us. The best we can do is try to steer in a particular direction.

I think the hardest part about being in your twenties is trying to figure out who you are and why you were put on this earth. Some people have an idea about what they want to do for a living and fight to do it. Others might enter a family business and learn to grow into their role. But for the majority of us, we have no earthy idea what the future holds. We must figure out what we want to do to succeed and survive. The world has so many expectations about what you're supposed to have accomplished by a certain age. When you don't feel like you are at the right phase in your life, you may end up feeling lost and confused, like you don't have a purpose. You may feel anxiety, confusion, frustration, or question the meaning of life.

Young adults are stuck in a conundrum. We are constantly faced with questions about natural adult development. We ask ourselves what we are doing with our lives. For most of us, life never has an *"Aha! I figured it all out!"* moment. And being in this world where incomes are stagnant and debt is soaring, our generation has put much on hold. *"I can't get married! How can I afford such an event? I can't have a baby! I can barely take care of myself. I can't buy a house! I don't even make enough to contribute to my IRA! Wait, what exactly is a IRA? I don't want a credit card; I am already in enough debt!"*

We ask ourselves if we are living up to our potential. This is not unusual, as every generation before us has experienced similar obstacles and had their own decades of social, economic, and emotional problems. It's hard to create a plan when you don't know exactly what you want to do as a career. It's hard to create a plan when it's not so easy to find that first job. But maybe that initial life plan doesn't have to be the be-all and end-all. Our twenties are meant to be about trial and error. Our twenties are about learning and growing into the people we are meant to be. These are perplexing times, and that's just the way it will always be.

The "quarter life crisis" should not be regarded as a negative experience. It is about realistically questioning what you have created in your life already, and asking yourself if you could achieve more by choosing different goals or career paths. For many Millennials, just making money is no longer an acceptable goal. We want our lives and careers to have some kind of meaning and social impact, which is why we tend to overthink or isolate ourselves in our confusion. Becoming an adult is about learning to set your own timelines, not trying to match your parents' or friends' achievements. No timeline is set in stone on how or what course your life has to take. You will realize that everyone else is also struggling with the "next steps." You can figure out who you are by traveling, exercising, making art, reading, writing, volunteering, meeting new people or stepping outside your comfort zone. The "quarter life crisis" is a new term for what we could just call "life."

There comes a point when you are financially and emotionally burdened and you start to lash out and blame society, your friends, your studies, the economy, anything really, for the position that you find yourself in. When I didn't have a job, I didn't feel complete. I didn't feel like I was living up to my full potential and I went into a state of sadness and loneliness for a while. I remember reading stories online of people who were unemployed for months to years who contemplated suicide as an end to the whirlwind of unhappiness surrounding them. This is a real issue for many who struggle with tough times, and it is heartbreaking to know that some people just don't know how to pull through to the other side. Not having money or a purpose is one of the most stressful situations in the world, and for some it can lead to total depression.

It's hard to envision what your next step is when you are busy worrying about money. Money comes and goes, but who you are will stick with you. Throughout the struggles in my twenties I learned that the time will pass regardless, so take some time out of your busy schedule to "do you," because it will pan out in the long haul. Maybe you have to settle for a little while. Maybe you have to do a job or work with people you do not like. Maybe you need that humbling experience to help you fully become the person you are meant to be. Maybe you have to fight a little harder than you ever thought you would. But it makes an achievement sweeter when you know that you fought for it.

Some of us take longer than others to figure things out, and that's okay. Ignore negative thoughts and comments from others, but do not ignore the facts. If you want something to show for yourself, you have to make the most of your time. Don't get me wrong, it's great to indulge in a lazy day, binge watching Netflix shows and stroking your... kitty cat... but the more time misspent, is time you will wish you had not wasted while young.

Even though having a job is a vital part of life, we must remember that we were not put on this planet *just* to work. We are here to have experiences, travel, make connections, and shape the world into a better place. Sure, we must pay the bills, but we also must find our passions deep down inside. If you're lucky enough to find work that makes you happy *and* contributes to society or a cause, then you achieved the dream!

When I was unemployed, I had ideas about what I could do to make a change within myself to be happy. I wrote more. I spent more time with my family. I watched and absorbed information on subjects I wanted to learn more about. I exercised, volunteered, and I wrote out my personal goals on paper. I wanted to give my days a purpose, even if I was not working at a full-time job. I couldn't waste time being lost and confused. I needed to make my life worth something, and not let myself wither in my own self-pity. I had to find the humor in rocky moments. Maybe I was a little disillusioned by society when set forth to find a career. But I kept looking for the right job, and found ways to pay the bills in the meantime. I may have been unlucky in my job search for years, but I knew eventually things just had to work out.

I have struggled, but I have also grown so much with each passing year. My 25th birthday was the first that I finally had a job that paid all the bills (while it lasted). I bought my first new car, and decided to throw myself a party to celebrate such a milestone. I booked a suite at the Gaylord Texan Resort and had 20 of my friends dressed in cocktail attire join me in dancing the night away at the Glass Cactus Nightclub. I wore a bright pink dress with silver sequined shoes and my hair done up in curls. It was my way of taking life by the horns and letting go of my worries for an evening. I was surrounded by people who cared about me—people trying to find their purpose in life, too. And though I knew I hadn't figured it all out yet, I learned enough to know that we should celebrate along the way.

I knew something was up with this whole "adulting" thing when my birthday presents from my parents were not exactly normal birthday wish list items: a bridesmaid dress, a trip to the vet for my cat, or a new car battery, or even… nothing at all. Oh, how life was so much simpler when all I ever worried about for my birthday was if there was enough cake and ice cream. Now I deal with getting *both* wrinkles *and* pimples! *How old am I again?*

I often find myself mulling over just how much life can change in the years after graduation. Time seems to fly faster. People come and go. Life throws challenges on every front: health, relationships, and financial responsibilities. I realize now life can throw us some pretty unsavory circumstances, but it is how we choose to handle those circumstances that makes all the difference. I am in charge of putting together my own life puzzle. And dare I say, as I grow older and push 30, and gain experience and knowledge, some parts of life just seem to fit right into place, while other puzzle pieces still remain scattered around.

It took me a while to find my balance and happiness. It took being poor and blowing through my savings account. It took living with my parents, applying to hundreds of jobs, working several crazy jobs, meeting different people, reading a ton of articles and books, and going through self-revelations, and gaining experience, to figure out what would allow me to feel whole.

My story isn't wrapped into a tight pretty bow. I still have a lot of figuring out to do, but my pursuits are not trivial. I finally landed a job as a project manager which utilizes my organizational and people skills *(thank the heavens, hallelujah!)*, provides work-life balance and travel, a cause to help people, and health insurance! After all the setbacks I endured, I now have a savings account. I have been able to take vacations to fun places like both Portlands, San Francisco, Sedona and Jamaica. I also find time to write! And yes, I *finally* moved out of my parents' house with my big orange kitty, Oliver. I also found love again, and we are set to be married in the fall of 2018!

It seems weird to be excited about being a normal grown-up, but I am. I've become a fully functioning, tax contributing, productive member of society! A society I hope to be a part of changing for the better. And I know deep down that with enough effort, more advancement can happen. I still sometimes feel like a lost, wandering cat, but other days I feel like I am on just the right path.

About The Author

Kristin D. Butler studied and practiced journalism and sociology while attending college in Fort Worth, Texas. Her generation's affairs are her beat. When she is not writing or reading, you can find her drinking sparkling wine, petting her cat's belly, and making up new words, dances and silly jingles.

Photo by Blake Bethel

Be social! Also, go check out pictures of my two cute cats, Oliver and (the newest addition) Eevee!

thecatsbeunemployed.com

facebook.com/thecatsbeunemployed

instagram.com/thecatsbeunemployed

Acknowledgements

Thank you, to my friends, exes, and co-workers whose stories or antidotes I used for this book. I changed some of your names, but you know who you are. Your stories will help others to not feel alone.

Thank you, Deborah Steinberg, my "book doctor" for challenging me and helped me grow in my vision quest.

Thank you, Julie Schoen, Cindy Draughon, and Julie Ortiz for your hard work editing and cleaning up this book.

Thank you, Noh A, for taking my ideas and bringing it all to life in beautiful illustrations.

Thank you to my parents, Kelley and Gaylon, and my sister, Hayley, for standing beside me and encouraging my thought processes.

Thank you to my other half, Luke, for your edits, ideas and support!

Thank you, my dear friend, Lauren, for reading some of my initial drafts, and helping me find the humor in things.

Thank you, Despot and Klughaus, for being inspired to concoct that bright yellow cat shirt, leading to much inspiration for this book.

Thank you, Oliver, for walking into my life my senior year of college, and for being the inspiration for the book artwork. Such a great cat and side-kick!

Dear Cool Cat,

Thank you for reading my book!! It means the world to me!

If, when reading this book, you related to any part, learned something new, laughed, cried, screamed, jumped up and down, spun on your head, or wanted to take several shots of whiskey . . . please do me a favor and write a review online and help spread the word. As an aspiring writer, I can only hope to thrive if readers like you encourage others to give this book a chance. With emotion comes action, and vice versa.

Clinks glass of champagne

Cheers!

Kristin

Bibliography

1. Rash Baum, William K. "12 Held in Sale of Pest Poisons, One 60 Times as Potent as the Legal Limit." *The New York Times* online, 9 September 2011.

2. Barello, Stephanie. "Consumer spending and U.S. employment from the 2007–2009 recession through 2022." Monthly Labor Review. U.S. Bureau of Labor Statistics, October 2014. Web.

3. Center on Budget and Policy Priorities. "Chart Book: The Legacy of the Great Recession." Retrieved from: http://www.cbpp.org/research/economy/chart-book-the-legacy-of-the-great-recession

4. Ruetschlin, Catherine, and Tamara Draut. "Stuck: Young America's Persistent Jobs Crisis." Demos.org, 2013. Web.

5. Jacobe, Dennis. "In U.S., Fewer Young Adults Holding Full-Time Jobs in 2013." Gallup.com, 26 July 2013. Web.

6. Lauff, E., and, S.J. Ingels. "Education Longitudinal Study of 2002 (ELS: 2002): A First Look at 2002 High School Sophomores 10 Years Later." NCES 2014-363. U.S. Department of Education and National Center for Education Statistics, January 2014.

7. Taylor, P., et al. "Young, underemployed and optimistic: Coming of age, slowly, in a tough economy." Pewsocialtrends.org. Pew Research Center, 9 February 2011. Web.

8   Accenture Strategy. "Are You The Weakest Link? Strengthening Your Talent Acquisition Strategy: Insights from the Accenture Strategy 2015 U.S. College Graduate Employment Study." Accenture.com, 2015. Web.

9   Kuhn and Mansour. "Is Internet Job Search Still Ineffective?" Econ. ucsb.edu. Economics Department of UCSB, 29 July 2013. Web.

10 Von Wachter, Till. "Young Workers: In a Wage Rut for Years." *The New York Times* online, 25 May 2011.

11 Hart Research Associates. "It takes more than a major: employer priorities for college learning and student success." *Liberal Education*. Vol. 99, No. 2. Spring 2013.

12 Generation Opportunity. "Youth Unemployment at 15.5% in April." Generationopportunity.org, 2 May 2014. Web.

13 "So How Many Millennials Are There in the US, Anyway?" Marketingcharts.com, 15 May 2017. Web.

14 Abel, Jaison, Richard Deitz, and Yaqin Su. "Are Recent College Grads Finding Good Jobs?" *Current Issues in Economics and Finance*. Volume 20. No. 1. Federal Reserve Bank of New York, 2014.

15 Leonhardt, David. "The Idled Young Americans." *The New York Times* online, 3 May 2013.

16 "2016 Workforce-Skills Preparedness Report." Payscale.com, 2016. Retrieved from: http://www.payscale.com/data-packages/job-skills

17 Sayed, Yusuf. "Making education a priority in the post-2015 development agenda: report of the Global Thematic Consultation on Education in the Post-2015 Development Agenda." Unicef.org. UNICEF and UNESCO, September 2013. Web.

18 "Committee on Incentives and Test-Based Accountability in Public Education at the National Research Council." Nap.edu, 2011. Web.

19 Tim Walker. "PISA 2009: U.S. Students in the Middle of the Pack." Neatoday.org, 7 December 2010. Web.

20 Strong American Schools. "Diploma to Nowhere." Paworldclassmath.webs.com, 2008. Web.

21 Wolfgang, Ben. "Scores show students aren't ready for college." *The Washington Times* online, 17 August 2011.

22 Jamrisko, Michelle, and Ilan Kolet. "Cost of college degree in US soars 12 fold: Chart of the day." *Bloomberg News* online, 15 August 2012.

23 Jesse, Detroit, David. "Government projects to make $50B in student loan profit." *USA TODAY* online, 16 June 2013.

24 Oliff, Phil, et al. "Recent Deep State Higher Education Cuts May Harm Students and the Economy for Years to Come." Cppp.org. Center on Budget and Policy Priorities, 19 March 2013. Web.

25 Baum, Sandy and Jennifer Ma. "Trends in College Pricing 2014." Collegeboard.org, 2014. Web.

26 Desrochers, Donna M., and Rita J. Kirshstein. "College Spending in a Turbulent Decade: Findings from the Delta Cost Project. A Delta

Data Update, 2000-2010." Deltacostproject.org. Delta Cost Project at American Institutes for Research, 2012. Web.

27 National Center for Education Statistics. "Undergraduate Enrollment." Nces.org, May 2016. Web.

28 National Center for Public Policy and Higher Education. "Two-Thirds Believe Qualified Students Are Being Shut Out of College." Publicagenda.org, 4 February 2009. Web.

29 The Pell Institute for the Study of Opportunity in Higher Education. "Indicators of Higher Education Equity in the United States." Pellinstitute.org, 2016. Web.

30 Center for American Progress. "The Middle-Class Squeeze." Cdn.americanprogress.org, September 2014. Web.

31 Mettler, Suzanne. *Degrees of Inequality: How the Politics of Higher Education Sabotaged the American Dream.* New York: Basic Books, a Member of the Perseus Group, 2014. Print.

32 US Department of Education. "Obama Administration Takes Action to Protect Americans from Predatory, Poor-Performing Career Colleges." Ed.gov, 14 March 2014. Web.

33 "Revealed: Google's Biggest Advertiser Is the University of Phoenix Spending Nearly $200,000 Every Day." Dailymail.com. Associated Newspapers, 31 October 2012. Web.

34 Lewin, Tamar. "Senate committee report on for-profit colleges condemns costs and practices." *The New York Times* online, 29 July 2012.

35 Johnson, Anne, Tobin Van Ostern, and Abraham White. "The student debt crisis." Americanprogress.org. Washington: Center for American Progress, 25 October 2012. Web.

36 Senate HELP Committee. "For Profit Higher Education: The Failure to Safeguard the Federal Investment and Ensure Student Success." Help.senate.gov. United States Senate, 30 July 2012. Web.

37 Hamilton, Justin. "Obama Administration Announces New Steps to Protect Students from Ineffective Career College Programs." Federalregister.gov. United States Government, 2 June 2011. Web.

38 "U.S. Department of Education Heightens Oversight of Corinthian Colleges." Federalregister.gov. United States Government, 19 June 2014. Web.

39 Fain, Paul. "Regulating Job Placement." Insidehighered.com, 17 April 2015. Web.

40 Corinthian Colleges. "Corinthian Announces Cessation of Effectively All Operations" *Business Wire* online, 26 April 2015.

41 U.S. Department of Education. "U.S. Department of Education Announces Path for Debt Relief for Students at 91 Additional Corinthian Campuses." Federalregister.gov. United States Government, 26 March 2016. Web.

42 U.S. Department Of Education. "Unofficial Notice of Proposed Rulemaking to Amend Direct Loan. . ." Federalregister.gov. United States Government, 16 June 2016. Web.

43 Douglas-Gabriel, Danielle. "Obama administration plans to overhaul rules on student debt forgiveness." *The Washington Post* online, 19 August 2015.

44 Pyke, Alan. "A Pool Of Sharks': Why For-Profit Colleges Are Descending On Shuttering Corinthian Campuses." Thinkprogress.org, 30 April 2015. Web.

45 Rosenbaum, James E., Regina Deil-Amen, and Ann E. Person. *After Admission: From College Access to College Success*. New York: Russell Sage Foundation, 2009. Print.

46 "2014 Retention/Completion Summary Tables." Act.org, 2014. Web.

47 Chopra, Rohit. "A closer look at the trillion." Consumerfinance.gov. Consumer Financial Protection Bureau, 5 August 2013. Web.

48 Kaplan, David. "The draconian hidden penalty on student loans." *Fortune* online, 10 May 2012.

49 "Presidential Memorandum -- Federal Student Loan Repayments." Obamawhitehouse.archives.gov, 9 June 2014. Web.

50 "Education at a Glance 2012: Highlights." Oecd.org. The Organisation for Economic Co-operation and Development, 2012. Web.

51 Arum, Richard, and Josipa Roksa. *Academically adrift: Limited learning on college campuses*. University of Chicago Press, 2011. Print.

52 "Young, Underemployed and Optimistic." Pewsocialtrends.org. Pew Research Center, 9 February 2013. Web.

53 Motel, Seth. "6 facts about marijuana." Pewresearch.org. Pew Research Center, 7 April 2014. Web.

54 "28 Legal Medical Marijuana States and DC. Laws, Fees, and Possession Limits." Procon.org, 28 December 2016. Web.

55 Silbaugh, Larson. "Distribution of Marijuana Tax Revenue." Issue Brief Number 15-10. Colorado.gov. Colorado Legislative Council Staff, July 2015. Web.

56 U.S. Congress Joint Economic Committee. "The Case for Maintaining Unemployment Insurance: Supporting Workers and Strengthening the Economy." Jec.senate.gov, 15 December 2011. Web.

57 O'Brien, Matthew. "The terrifying reality of long-term unemployment." *The Atlantic* online, 13 April 2013.

58 Schmitt, John. "This is the year minimum wage peaked. The Minimum Wage is Too Damn Low." Cepr.net. Center for Economic and Policy Research, March 2012. Web.

59 DeNavas-Walt, Carmen and Bernadette D. Proctor. "Income, poverty, and health insurance coverage in the United States: 2013." P60-249. Census.gov. Diane Publishing, September 2014. Web.

60 "The Low-Wage Recovery: Industry Employment and Wages Four Years into the Recovery." Nelp.org. National Employment Law Project, April 2014. Web.

61 "The Effects of a Minimum-Wage Increase on Employment and Family Income." Cbo.gov. Congressional Budget Office, 18 February 2014. Web.

62 "The 2016 Deloitte Millennial Survey: Winning over the next generation of leaders." Deloitte Touche Tohmatsu Limited, 2016. Retrieved from: www.2.deloitte.com/global/en/pages/about-deloitte/articles/millennialsurvey.html

63 Seppanen, Sally, and Wendy Gualtieri. "The millennial generation research review." Uschamberfoundation.org. US Chamber of Commerce, 12 November 2012. Web.

64 Belle, Deborah and Heather E. Bullock. "Psychological Effects of Unemployment and Underemployment." Spssi.org. The Society for the Psychological Study of Social Issues. Unknown date. Web.

65 Morin, Rich, and Rakesh Kochhar. "Lost Income, Lost Friends--and Loss of Self-Respect." Pewsocialtrends.org. Pew Research Center, 22 July 2010. Web.

66 Cappelli, Peter. "The skills gap myth: Why companies can't find good people." *Time Magazine* online, 4 June 2012.

67 Vikki, Wachino, Samantha, Artiga, and Robin Rudowitz. "How is the ACA Impacting Medicaid Enrollment?" Kff.org. Kaiser Family Foundation, 5 May 2014. Web.

68 "Office on Women's Health Report to the White House Council on Women and Girls." Womenshealth.gov. Department of Health and Human Services, November 2009. Web.

69 Becker, Nora V., and Daniel Polsky. "Women saw large decrease in out-of-pocket spending for contraceptives after ACA mandate removed cost sharing." *Health Affairs* 34.7, 1204-1211. 2015.

70   Hill, Catey. "10 Most Expensive Cities in America to Have a Child." Marketwatch.com, 30 September 2017. Web.

71   Truven Health Analytics. "The Cost of Having a Baby in the United States." January 2013. Retrieved from: http://transform.childbirthconnection.org/reports/cost/

72   "Out-of-pocket Maximum Limits on Health Plans." Obamacarefacts.com. Web.

73   Cohen, Robin A., and Michael E. Martinez. "Health insurance coverage: Early release of estimates From the National Health Interview Survey, January–March 2012." Cdc.gov. Centers for Disease Control and Prevention, 2012. Web.

74   Collins, Sara R., et al. "Young, uninsured, and in debt: why young adults lack health insurance and how the Affordable Care Act is helping." Issue Brief from Commonwealth Fund, 2012.

75   Caldwell, Nolan, et al. "How much will I get charged for this? Patient charges for top ten diagnoses in the emergency department." PloS one 8.2 e55491. 2013.

76   Tamkins, Theresa. "Medical bills prompt more than 60 percent of US bankruptcies." CNN Health online, 5 June 2009.

77   "Key facts about the uninsured population." Kff.org. Kaiser Family Foundation, September 2016. Web.

78   Commonwealth Fund. "Three-quarters of those who have lost jobs and health insurance are skipping needed health care." Sciencedaily.com, 24 August 2011. Web.

79 "Medicaid expansion & what it means for you." Retrieved from https://www.healthcare.gov/medicaid-chip/medicaid-expansion-and-you

80 Merritt Hawkins. "A Survey of America's Physicians: Practice Patterns and Perspectives." Physiciansfoundation.org, September 2012. Web.

81 Annalisa, Merelli. "Charted: Adopting universal health coverage just makes economic sense." Qz.com. Atlantis Media Co., 12 December 2014. Web.

82 Nadia, Kounang. "Why pharmaceuticals are cheaper abroad." CNN online, 28 September 2015.

83 Ventola, C. Lee. "Direct-to-consumer pharmaceutical advertising: therapeutic or toxic?" Pharmacy and Therapeutics 36.10, 669. 2011.

84 Addati, Laura, Naomi Cassirer, and Katherine Gilchrist. "Maternity and Paternity at Work. Law and Practice around the World." Ilo.org. International Labour Organization, 2014. Web.

85 The Council of Economic Advisers. "The Economics of Paid and Unpaid Leave." Whitehouse.gov, June 2014. Web.

86 Williams, Joan C., and Heather Boushey. "The three faces of work-family conflict: The poor, the professionals, and the missing middle." Americanprogress.org, 25 January 2010. Web.

87 Kiersten, Schmidt and Sarah Almukhtar. "Where Women's Marches Are Happening around the World." *The New York Times* online, 20 January 2017.

88 Easley, Jason. "Women's March Is The Biggest Protest In US History As An Estimated 2.9 Million March." Politicus USA, 21 January 2017. Web.

89 World Economic Forum. "The Global Gender Gap Report 2016." Reports.weforum.org, 2016. Web.

90 The Center for Responsive Politics. Retrieved from: https://www.opensecrets.org/lobby/top.php?indexType=i

91 Fry, Richard. "Millennials surpass Gen Xers as the largest generation in U.S. labor force." Pew research.org. Pew Research Center, 11 May 2015. Web.

92 The Execu|Search Group. "2017 HIRING OUTLOOK: Strategies for engaging with today's talent and improving the candidate experience." 2017. Retrieved from: http://www.execu-search.com/~/media/Resources/pdf/2017_Hiring_Outlook_eBook

93 Nittono H, Fukushima M, Yano A, Moriya H. "The Power of Kawaii: Viewing Cute Images Promotes a Careful Behavior and Narrows Attentional Focus." PLoS ONE 7(9): e46362. 26 September 2012.

650.14 BUT
Butler, Kristin D.
The cats be unemployed
: a Millennial's

05/03/18

Somerville Public Library
35 W. End Ave.
Somerville, NJ 08876
908-725-1336